At the Feet of Serenity

EVE GWARTNEY

authorHOUSE®

AuthorHouse™
1663 Liberty Drive
Bloomington, IN 47403
www.authorhouse.com
Phone: 1 (800) 839-8640

Published by AuthorHouse   02/22/2016

ISBN: 978-1-5049-6694-8 (sc)
ISBN: 978-1-5049-6707-5 (e)

Print information available on the last page.

Dedicated to Derek Clayland and his posterity.

Prologue

Journal Entry by Henry Clayland: August 10, 1934
Sweetheart: We had a very enjoyable walk and talk
tonight. Afterwards we went over and sat at the feet of
old Serenity in Euclid Park. Remember, dear, I bought
you a bouquet of gladiolas as a token of my love.

A small cinder-block house, a rushing stream beyond it, and a terraced slope between the house and the stream comprised the Clayland family home site. The stream gushed with the watershed of mountain snow melted from the nearby mountain that defined the valley and its geological perspective. Henry and Jensine Clayland had bonded to the land and its purpose. The terraced slope was saturated with vegetation which was tenderly maintained by Jensine. The flourishing fruit trees had been planted by Henry's hands the season he and Jensine arrived to begin a new phase of their lives together. Observant motorists passing by the property favorably judged the owners as being people who cared about the potential of a small plot of earth.

A man's home is his castle and everything is relative. The cinder-block house was the implicit statement of the financial success that Henry had shared with Jensine, his wife of thirty-one years. There were two bedrooms on the ground level, a living room where one could comfortably visit, and a kitchen that was large enough to work without a struggle. The most sensational feature of the house was the flushing toilet, for they had gone without one in the years that were behind them. The unfinished section of the basement held the washing machine amongst stacked boxes of unremembered things. There were three basement bedrooms that had been formed from studs and discounted paneling. The house was a worthy status that Henry and Jensine thought they would never achieve. Although he was now in a state of immortality, one basement room was still reserved for Henry. It was space that held his possessions, undisturbed since the time of his demise.

Henry got buried in the cemetery that was within walking distance from the house. It made it convenient for Jensine to walk there and put roses from her rose garden whenever she felt the desire to pay tribute to his memory. She had a reserved spot next to him for the time when she too would make the great transition. Her conscience was slightly challenged knowing that she would have the place of honor next to him instead of Grace. Grace, Henry's first wife, had claimed the privilege the year before Jensine and Henry married. A grave for Henry's future had been purchased with Grace's at the time of her funeral arrangements. Because Henry was buried elsewhere, the grave-site next to Grace was destined to remain unoccupied, to be donated, or to be sold to a stranger. Jensine's justification for the action of burying Henry down the road was a reasonable one: she was married to Henry longer than Grace had been.

Jensine acquired the title "Mamma" one year, four months and three days after Grace, contributor to my DNA, fell off the earth. Jensine became Mamma since the day I turned sixteen months, for that was the day that my father, Henry, married her.

Ashamed cordiality and awkward conversation dominated our first few hours together on a fall day in 1994. Mamma began, "How have you been all these years, Camilla? Now what are the names of your children?"

My father's image and his purpose stayed with me during the time that he was alive and the time that he wasn't. As a child I found no fault in him, for I knew no reason why I should. Later in life, when I gained the wisdom that comes from battered experiences, I concluded that he was smart about some things and not smart about others; he was determined about some things and not determined about others. As I grew taller he grew shorter, and the protector in him seemed to fade away.

Although he was dead, I went to my father's home to connect with him again. A dimly lit basement room brought the bright comfort that comes when a connection is made with the memory of the immortal. My father's histories, preserved as he had left them, lingered in a room of reminiscence within a small cinder-block house. To someone without any connections to my father the basement room would have seemed just a dreary basement room, void of any soul. I felt warmth in the basement where someone else might have felt a chill.

When he was living he was a man who was caught in the spirit of Elijah. Elijah was a prophet of the Bible who was the advocate for the bonding of families when the Lord stated the grave command for turning the "heart of the fathers to the children, and the heart of the children to the fathers." The Lord's strong condemnation to both Jew and Gentile was imprinted within the Old Testament, burned into the last two verses of the Book of Malachi.

For as long as I can remember, my father researched names of his ancestors. He recorded the information onto pedigree charts and family group sheets. Little notes here and there, about this or that person who lived so long ago, who passed along a few genes here and there to whatever extent the line reached into the yonder years. He stored his notes and his information in three or four filing cabinets: the ones now crammed into the corner waiting for a curious member of his posterity to access it. That day I swept the pages of recorded words, scattered letters and journals of wonder. I rambled through boxes of his photos, faces of the years beyond me. The warmth in the basement that was caused by his heart calmed the anger of my youth, anger which Henry Clayland had been so much a part of. I brought him back to me from the enlightenment he left behind.

One photograph that I found was of my father standing in front of a statue. Dad was dependable when it came to labeling his records: Henry Clayland, 1934, Washington DC. It wasn't any clearer than that. I could see the faint impression of the letter E at the base of the statue, but it was turned the wrong way. Daddy once had a darkroom so he could develop his photographs. He must have flipped the negative as he put it into the chemicals.

The statue was not identified, but she was a curious image. She had a homely kind of beauty; a hint of Greek, I thought, from what I knew about Greek, or what Hollywood knew about Greek. Through an act of curiosity, I had previously discovered that her name was Serenity. It was a curiosity most likely caused by deprivation. Serenity, my ensign of hope, the symbol of what once was, and what should be, became mine to make meaningful.

Another photograph was slightly warped with time: a black and white portrayal of Henry Clayland's five young children, taken when I was a few months old. I was sitting on the lap of my brother Tom, a curly haired young man of twelve years smiling as though smiling was his duty. Annabelle took her place beside me and Tom, a full view of a small girl whose head must have been full of far-fetched wishes. Carl was the toddler who appeared uncertain as to the reason why he was supposed to stand still. He wasn't much older than me. Derek was the little boy sitting on the ground with his mouth puckered for a whistle. Knowing Derek he wasn't going to allow anything to interfere with his plans. A father and one little son posed for the capture of a flash in time. In the future they shared a common plight.

An advertisement for the sale of a hotel caught my attention. An 8 x 11 inch glossy black and white photograph of the hotel was stapled to the description of the property. It was the hotel my parents had owned at the time of my birth, and it was also my first home: Route 66, Winslow, Arizona. I read each feature of the property and the reason the hotel went on the market. Living quarters large enough to accommodate a small family might have been appealing to a local entrepreneur. The explanation for the sale was an abstract appeasement to the demands for a stable existence, an existence longed for but never quite found…

One

Henry and Grace Clayland owned and operated the Desert Edge Hotel on Main Street in Winslow. The city, proudly nested upon historic Route 66, invited entry into deserts, cities, valleys, and expectations beyond them. The weary travelers emerging from the cities eastward and westward kept the bookkeeper busy throughout the seasons. A few of the hotel patrons were permanent residents who paid their rent on a week-to-week arrangement.

The Clayland family lived in an apartment that was converted from four hotel rooms at the end of the complex. Though it was small, the home fulfilled its purpose. Like most people, Grace and Henry worked hard and liked to think of better times ahead. The dry air of the daytime was therapeutic and there was no war in the land or abroad. The vast array of stars at night furnished a sense of comfort in the desert town.

A few nights after Thanksgiving, the dippers were in their December positions. The baying coyotes below them would not relent. Their howls were louder than usual, the evening was chillier than usual, and the night was darker than usual. Grace and Henry's five children waited anxiously for the return of their mother, who was lying on a hospital bed. She was far from home, but only because she had to be.

While in the hospital Grace managed to pick up a pencil and a piece of paper to write a letter to her family. Then she asked someone to mail it to her home. As Henry read the letter to his children they no longer feared the coyotes. Their mother was there for a few minutes in the room that once languished. At the close of her letter: *with all my love, Mother*, she vanished again.

> *My Dearest Henry and Children:*
> *You can't imagine how anxious I am to see you and have us all together again. I'm sure this will be our happiest Christmas because we'll all be together again. We can make all kinds of candy and pretty butterflies and popcorn balls. And I'll make a real English plum pudding for Christmas dinner.*
> *Tom, I love you, and Derek, and Annabelle, and Carl even more (if that's possible) since we got our new little girl. She surely is sweet, and I know you'll love her very much. Henry, all the nurses felt so badly when they learned it was you who asked to see the baby Saturday. They said to tell you it was just a misunderstanding, and they would have brought her out to you special.*
> *I worry about you all taking colds up there in that cold weather. Do be careful. Be careful of Carl getting out the back doors and I hope you won't build fires in the fireplace until I get there. I'm so afraid*

Carl will get into the hot ashes after the fire
has gone out.
    This pencil point has about worn flat.
Just remember, I love you terribly much and
I dream and think of you all the time.
    It's four o'clock. I have supper at five,
and I get the baby at six, which is one of the
highlights of my day. The other highlights
are the other two times that I get her.
    With all my love, Mother

The children knew that she would come back, and she did. She found the strength to write a letter to her parents. The written word, entrusted to the mail system, kept the communication flowing. Her parents read the letter, responded to it, then folded the letter Grace had written, and put it in a box of letters that were noteworthy to save. After their daughter's death, they gave it to Henry so that their grandchildren could learn about their mother. ***The written word is truth, knowledge, and fortune, especially for those who are left behind.***

As Henry prepared the evening meal for the family, he listened for the bell that would signal a new customer for his business. He was always prepared to drop everything and drag a child or two to the front desk, take care of registration, and revert back to the necessary domestic work. He put forth his best effort at meeting the demands of his stewardships in the home and in the business. I was the newborn that Grace wrote home about.

In amounts proportional to the size and eating habits of each child, Henry spooned the food onto four plates. "It's time to say the blessing on the food." The kids knew what was expected when a prayer over the food was said. "Be quiet, fold your arms in reverence, don't kick your brother, and listen to what is being said. When you say 'amen' it means you are agreeable."

Henry proceeded. "Dear Heavenly Father, bless this food and bless Mommy that she will get better. Amen." It was a short prayer but Daddy had a lot to do that evening.

"Amen," repeated Derek confidently. He was a lively little boy of six years.

"Amen," repeated Annabelle, with less boldness than her brother. Annabelle was four years old so it was natural for her to want her mommy near her at all times. She felt a little puzzled. She didn't understand some things, but she was learning.

Tom stretched his leg under the table and kicked the chair across from him. He was irritated because Mother wasn't with them. Sometimes it was difficult to say anything to the Lord above, not even an "Amen."

Little Carl was just learning to talk so his "amen" came out missing the first syllable. They didn't expect much more from a seventeen-month-old.

Henry's domestic efforts extended into the nighttime, the daytime, the afternoon, and the times he used to think existed. Time was of the essence and it could beat you down.

Night fell and the kids were in bed at last. It was time for him to look in on Grace and bring her something to eat. He entered the makeshift kitchen, quickly washed the dinner dishes and prepared her meal. With a weary gait he stumbled down the hall toward the bedroom, then paused in his approach. He felt something was wrong when Grace didn't respond to the creaking of the door or the sudden illumination of the light that quickly erased the darkness of nightfall. He slowly approached their bed to avoid startling her. A closed Venetian blind on the window, a hard tiled floor, and the absence of unnecessary furniture allowed her raspy breath to echo. Perspiration dripped from Grace's face and mocked the cool temperature of the room. Her face was ashen. He knew that his responsibility to Grace would need to be brief. He sat on the edge of the bed and nudged her out of haziness. "Dear, I brought you something to eat."

Between the strains of her harsh inhalations, Grace sorrowed and despaired. In silence she objected to the food, the incapacitated state she was in, and the sinking state of her health and well-being. She objected to the broken promises she made to her children: together they would make candy, popcorn balls and pretty butterflies. She noticed when Henry turned on the light but she had no strength to acknowledge it.

"Dear, I'll be back to check on you in a few minutes."

By the time the children awoke, their friend Violet was already in the home scurrying around helping with the preparations of Grace's trip to the hospital, a trip that Henry insisted upon. Carl toddled into his mother's bedroom. The little toddler's angelic face peered over the mattress to greet his mother. His little hands reached out to the bed sheets. He bent his knees to maneuver himself onto the bed. It was a natural thing for any little boy that was especially fond of his mother. Grace found enough strength in her arms to position them for a lingering hug. She kissed him sweetly on his plump little cheeks that invited the tenderness that comes with kisses. Annabelle came into the room next. When she saw her mother she ran to her, climbed onto the bed with more skill than her little brother and cuddled up beside her. Grace ran her fingers through her daughter's hair. She had splendid thoughts of raising her to maturity and being there for her through most of the stages of her life. Grace had thoughts of being a grandmother and a great grandmother, and beyond it. She and Henry grew old together in her mind.

Henry approached Grace to carry her outside. He lifted her from their bed without effort, for his arms were as strong as his love for her. He walked toward the door with her securely in his arms. Annabelle and Carl followed them as any two little children would whose mother was leaving them. I was somewhere in a room oblivious to the event. I'm sure that I was eager to make demands at my convenience.

Tom and Derek stood together in the narrow hallway as their father and mother swept by them. Despite the five-year difference in age, the two boys were as fond of each other as brothers can be. Tom was tolerant of his younger brother, who followed him around and often got in his way. Grace glanced over Henry's shoulder at her children. She looked into the eyes of Tom, who stood confidently. Being a young man, he was caught in the transition between irresponsibility and responsibility, between childhood and adulthood. He fought the fear that began to grip him but then remembered all the times she had been carried away. She would return to them as she always did.

"Take care of your brothers and sisters." His mother's words floated into Tom's ears and alarmed the child within him. Though Grace didn't know it at the time, they were her deathbed words. Her bed was the arm of her husband; her audience was her children, one of which was Derek. Derek was the other child who remembered her last words to them, and he took them into his innocent heart. To any little boys in a household where death was not eminent it was a harmless phrase: "take care of your brothers and sisters." But because death was eminent in the Clayland household, the words intended for Tom burned an ominous mark upon Derek as well.

With his soul-mate, wife, and mother to his five children in his arms, Henry stepped into the desert's winter wind. He placed Grace in the back seat of the car. Then he went back for me and placed me in a padded pasteboard box, for pasteboard boxes were once the cradle of the car. I was the privileged child that was selected to go with them on the final phase of our mother's journey on earth. My father got behind the wheel and began the sixty-mile journey back to the same hospital where they had been a few days earlier. It was the forties, when the highways were not expressways, and Route 66 was the super highway.

Grace closed her eyes and thought of the children she was leaving behind. She was afraid of what might lie ahead. She drifted into sleep and fell into her sea of hope. She dreamed.

The trip was dry and dusty as was the nature of trips through the desert. Grace slept except for the time that I cried. She, like most mothers, couldn't sleep through the cries of her child. She talked my father into letting her hold me. Henry stopped the car, handed me over the car seat, and laid me on my mother's lap. My mother gently rocked me. She tenderly touched my cheeks and stroked the softness of my hair as any mother would. I'm sure that I relished her touch. It was our last bonding moment.

She once had a dream that reached to me. When she dreamed the dream she was young and full of the future, the typical future that most young girls admired. But something wasn't right inside her. A tormenting kind of mystery had fallen on her. She wasn't like most young girls. Her doctor told her it was necessary to make adjustments to her goal of having children: the kind that would fall out of her. If she wanted them she would have to adopt them, take them from someone else's body and spirit. In the dream, a small child broke from a crowd of children. The child approached her in the shadows that dreams are made of. Then the child faded from her mind the moment sunlight swept over her eyes. It was a fleeting moment of a morning vision but it was a message that her dream would come true. She would have children, even if she had to adopt them.

She told Henry, before she married him, that she was as barren as they come. She told him on a Sunday on their walk home from Church in the persuasion of the park where they often walked. They went down the western slope where they could be alone. She told him at the feet of Serenity. In their love and common interests, they declared Serenity to be their favorite statue. They held Serenity's creator in high esteem. They appreciated his artistic gift and his willingness to share it. They went to Serenity often to talk and to be alone with their affection. Henry and Grace expected their insignia of love, devotion, commitment, and sacrifice, carved with a chisel and placed in a national park, would endure without malice or contempt.

Henry took his handkerchief from his pocket and spread it on the ground for her. They fell into each other's arms. The occasional neglected murmurs of automobiles on Sixteenth Street drowned into a crevice of silence. They could hear only the words they spoke to each other.

Henry professed his tender love to her, and he explained that her limitations did not sway his love. He told her that he was willing to adopt children. *At Serenity's feet love is unconditional.*

They married in the summer across the road from Serenity, where the Church's steeple cast its proud shadow near her. Stalwart, unbending, unwavering through strife, patient for the time when "wonderful" would happen.

Patience is a virtue. Good can be born from the bad if mankind strives hard enough for it. Medical science blessed Grace with a solution to her barrenness. A hormone therapy granted her the potential for motherhood. She begged to be treated, and she thanked God for those who made it possible.

I was conceived. Cells split the way the codes dictated. I hoarded the nourishment my mother allowed. And then I was born. My father placed me in my mother's arms after my cleaning, allowing his trembling hands to finally relax. My mother studied me, and then sighed as if to say, "It is enough." At the time, I was there only to take, and to demand a sacrifice of someone.

We were almost in Flagstaff.

Two

My father dropped me off at Aunt Charlotte's house. Aunt Charlotte was my father's sister and also Uncle Edwin's wife. A brother and a sister were married to a sister and a brother. Henry gave Grace a drink of water, then took her to the hospital. She was admitted in the late afternoon. Edwin was at the hospital working his assigned shift as a resident physician.

Edwin hadn't realized the seriousness of the new turn in his sister's illness, a waste of a chance to make her like she was in the springtime. The doctors decided Grace needed special treatment immediately. They arranged to have her go on intravenous fluids. Proper nutrition and plenty of fluids was the consensus. But the team wasn't going to take chances. Grace got admitted into Intensive Care where the nurses could watch her closely; and they all felt certain that the small and frail sister of Edwin would have a full recovery.

The halls were empty and silent when the alarm from Intensive Care went off. Edwin's confidence turned to stone when he remembered that Grace was the only patient in IC. He ran, stumbled, and tripped over his thoughts until he reached the unit. The Intensive Care nurses were in a state of panic.

Grace should not have had water in her stomach, an indulgence that seemed quite normal. For someone ill like Grace it might come up at a most inappropriate time. That is exactly what happened! If it happened to a healthy person it would have fallen into a pan or upon a pillow to be scooped up and washed, then forgotten about. The drink of water that Henry gave her slid into her lungs, aspirating her life away. If they had known, she wouldn't have consumed it. Her lungs experienced a violent abscessing, a destruction of delicate tissues that were meant for only the exchanges of the molecules in air and not to be shared with anything else.

Edwin fought to restore his melting composure. He lost the attempt when he saw his sister struggle to breathe and fight for air, air that was there but no longer promised help for her. Edwin turned around and darted into the hallway. He needed and demanded immediate assistance. Down the hallway he saw his colleagues come quickly towards him, tapping sounds on the hard floor. Though he knew they could not hear him he begged them to make the sounds come faster. Before they were in earshot he began his plea for help. He screamed as if death was at the door to whisk away his sister. "She'll die, I can't save her by myself. I need help." He made his co-workers realize the urgency of doing something for his sister. He stammered. "She can't die. She has children. She's my sister. She has to live."

At the side of the deathbed their learning was stilled and their anguish was stirred. A touch on her hand and a look of remorse were all they could offer. They knew that her pain soon would be finished, and that her spirit would leave her ravished body. Edwin's sense of professionalism vanished. He was no longer a physician. He became a little child begging for something he could never have. Hope was not possible. Begging did no good. Not even prayers could restore the battered proteins of her lungs.

"Edwin, we're so sorry. There is nothing we can do. You know that her lungs have been destroyed."

Death came for Grace in less than five minutes. Edwin's coworkers pined at the bedside after the transition of spirit was made. They reverently bowed their heads as a token of respect for the dead. And then they left to attend their duties. It was a bad day for everyone.

When my father placed me in the arms of my Aunt Charlotte he thanked her profusely for her acts of kindness in helping him and Grace through their difficult crisis.

It was the second day of the New Year. Henry waited in the hospital lounge to hear the prognosis. He was worried. Putting Grace into Intensive Care sent the message to him that her illness was serious, but the thought of losing her hadn't crossed his mind. Dealing with the burden of Grace's illness tasked his thoughts for the past several days. Death was too unreal, too mean, and too contradictory of an act of nature to happen to anyone so young, so needed, so beautiful, and so important.

A waiting room full of hard shiny clean walls and uncompromising benches wasn't a pleasant place to be when worried. Henry planned on staying until Grace was released from the ICU. The day began to close and a new one approached. The tedium of waiting peaked. The odors of the hospital began to dissipate. The harshness of the wall tiles diminished and their cold atmosphere turned moderate. The hard chair that Henry was sitting upon began to seem kind. His mind escaped into an eclipse of memories of how and why their lives came together. His memory floated back twenty years:

He is twenty years old. Responsibilities don't weigh on him like they do now. It is a time of his youth when goals are only an illusion and potential conquests are unlimited. To make his goals a reality is up to him. He has time. He is doing what is expected of him. He is giving two years of his life to his religion: the Church of Jesus Christ of Latter-day Saints. Serving a proselyting mission is expected of him, just as it has always been expected of every honorable young Mormon man. He is very fortunate to be called to South Africa. In his opinion it's the most interesting place in the world. South Africa is saturated with excitement and adventures. Wild beasts might appear at his very doorstep! South Africa abounds with tales of conquests and defeats in the history of its colonization.

He gazes upon a photograph of a beautiful girl. Her image speaks in tacit looks that are subtle to the heart. Her eyes look at him as if to say, "It's okay to be my sweetheart." Her lips invite affection and the softness of her oval face implies softness of her soul. The framed photograph sits on the desk of his companion, his assigned roommate, Elder Clemenson. The elder has a collection of photographs that almost any missionary would admire. One cherished picture is of his girlfriend who he is planning to marry one day. The remaining are photographs of his family members.

Grace, the girl in the photograph, is one of Elder Clemenson's sisters. The frame of the photo teases the edge of the desk, inviting a tumble onto the floor. His roommate makes it a habit of throwing his socks over her picture, a convenient location before retiring. The habit must end. "You should be ashamed of treating your sister so disrespectfully. She's too pretty for your old socks."

He steps from the ship anchored in the harbor at San Diego. His family is there to embrace him, then on to his native land of Arizona where he meets his friend and former companion, Elder Clemenson. An invitation for a visit begins his relationship with Grace.

His reverie traveled swiftly to the District of Columbia. The year was 1934.

Grace is employed as a secretary in the capitol city of the nation. At her insistence he follows her to the grand city, far away from home. The White House, the Capitol, the monuments, and the art are worthy to write home about. Mom and Dad want him on the farm for a few more years. They'll have to learn to thrive without him, for his life is now with Grace.

He desperately searches for employment. He fights the discouragement as he faces rejection. The country struggles to overcome a harrowing depression. The new president of Germany, Adolf Hitler, is planting the seeds of evil. Henry realizes that many people are worse off than he is. He finally does find employment after months of searching.

He meets her at her doorstep to begin their walk to Church. She reaches for his hand and steps into the Sunday sunlight. They enter the northeast entrance to their neighborhood park: a clean and tidy city block reserved for lush lawns, flower gardens, water fountains, and monuments. They pay little attention to the visitors who are there to stroll the pleasant paths. Their attentions are for each other. They leave the northwest corner and head north to where Sixteenth Street meets Columbia Road and Harvard. At the intersection they look upward at the Church's steeple. Upon its top, a statue of the Angel Moroni is trumpeting his message to the world. It's the only statue of him that is positioned upon a Church meetinghouse. The Angel Moroni, the Church's icon, is normally reserved for placement upon temples.

The Sunday Service is complete. They walk through the park, taking their time. Serenity is resting on the western slope of the park. A walking path welcomes patrons to come and partake of the sense of peace she has to offer. Henry and Grace sit on the ground and lean against Serenity's foundation. They talk of their plans for the future. They will be married in August.

The statue Serenity is their meeting place of preference. He poses in front of the statue as Grace captures on film the aristocratic beauty and gracefulness of Serenity. She hands his camera back to him. He photographs Grace as she poses against the gatepost at the northeast entrance to the park. Her age and her countenance are preserved for their history, and are promised to their posterity.

They exit the park at the south entrance. Wide sweeping stairways, located at opposite sides of the cascaded water fountain, end at the level of the reflecting pool. East of the reflecting pool are the Buchanan memorial and the Dante statue. Joan of Arc, the symbol of bravery, appears at the center of the park overlooking the flowing water fountains.

The sound of swift footsteps coming from a restricted hallway suddenly jolted Henry back into reality. The harsh surroundings of the hospital dimmed the vista of history in which he was savoring. His chair once more became institutionalized. The sounds of the footsteps bounced their echoes violently against the walls around him. The sound became swifter. He heard shouting. He thought the shouting came from Edwin. "What's happening?"

Grace wished she wasn't in the hospital but she was willing to go through any lengths and make any sacrifices to have her health restored. She was thankful for all those who were so important to her in her life: her family, her doctors, and her friends. Her brother Edwin once told her that she was the one that inspired him to become a physician.

Grace's thoughts wandered into her home filled with happy children. They were pleasant thoughts of being in her home with her children. An old year ended and invited a new one to begin, and it would continue for many years to come. Henry journeyed the years with her: the ones behind and the ones ahead. They all sang the usual childhood songs, they laughed together, and they gathered the ingredients together for the popcorn balls. The children liked the popcorn balls more than the candy; and then the butterflies of course...

Burning in her breath seized the moment with her children. Her thoughts began to get dizzy. Fire was burning and hurting her. The children faded. She needed more air, but it wouldn't come. She fought to inhale. The intense pressure became fierce. Pain in flames. Someone touched her hand. Crushing darkness from her brain; then the pain was gone.

"Edwin, I'm sorry."

Edwin forced his strained voice into a scream. "She isn't supposed to die. She has babies. She has children. She's my sister. She can't die." He was bewildered. "When will I wake up from this terrible nightmare?" His mind trembled. He kept waiting for the hallucination to end. "Wake up, Edwin. Wake up, Grace. Please wake up."

The nightmare was real. Shock twisted his thoughts as he attempted to grasp the last few minutes. He began to indulge himself in "ifs": "If only she had arrived earlier. If only I had been with her before it happened." He could have gone on forever with "ifs."

Then the tears came for a sister he had loved.

A few minutes passed. He wasn't able to face Henry, who was still waiting in the lounge. He tried to calm down. What was going to happen to her children? How could Henry manage without Grace? Grace was the stabilizing force in Henry's life. She was the one responsible for the success they were experiencing. She was his inspiration. Henry needed to be told, but how?

Edwin's knees weakened as he walked down the hall to tell Henry. He was almost at the door to the lounge. He turned around and went back into his office. He needed to be alone in his grief. He sent someone else to tell Henry.

Three

Carl and I weren't taken to the funeral. Annabelle, Derek, and Tom attended. The funeral centered on theological concepts meaningful to any Mormon who had a desire to return from whence he came. They were the same doctrines that stemmed from the Old and New Testaments of the Bible. They were concepts that many people were comfortable with regardless of their religious convictions.

The stained glass window of the Good Shepherd brought a temporary feeling of peace into the lives of those deeply affected by a woman's untimely death. The vocalization of the soloist softened the anguish of the mourners who grieved over a life cut short. The hymn, saturated with doctrines expounding the plan of happiness and the eternal nature of life, reminded the mourners of their glorious purposes:

"Oh, my father, thou that dwellest
in the high and glorious place.
When shall I regain thy presence,
and again behold thy face?
In thy holy habitation
did my spirit once reside?

In my first primeval childhood
was I nurtured near thy side?

For a wise and glorious purpose
thou hast placed me here on earth,
and withheld the recollection
of my former friends and birth.
Yet, oft-times, a secret something
whispered, 'You're a stranger here.'
And I felt that I had wandered
from a more exalted sphere.

I had learned to call thee father
through thy spirit from on high.
But, until the key of knowledge
was restored I knew not why.
In the heavens are parents single?
No, the thought makes reason stare.
Truth is reason; truth eternal
tells me I've a mother there.

When I leave this frail existence,
when I lay this mortal by,
Father, Mother, may I meet you
in your royal courts on high?
Then, at length, when I've completed
all you sent me forth to do,
With your mutual approbation,
let me come and dwell with you."

In the premortal-existence, the time before birth when our spirits lived with God, spirits were taught that sojourn on earth was necessary for their eternal progression and the fulfillment of their destinies. They rejoiced at the thought of gaining a tabernacle of flesh and blood at their assigned times on earth. At the time of birth, the veil, a kind of spiritual membrane, was created to blind their memories of their pre-mortal existence. Before mortal birth happened, the spirits were taught the purpose of life. The spirits learned that they would be faced with adversities in their mortal journeys. Adversities were to help the "blind" to gain sight and increase in wisdom. Knowledge and wisdom acquired on earth were to be carried into the next life.

Although the veil was drawn at birth, a light that everyone was born with whispered of a higher existence. This light was also called the conscience. Every person was blessed with this light when they gained their bodies of flesh and blood. Many people would shun it during their lifetimes, a choice endowed to them from on high. Agency, the ability and freedom to choose good or evil and that everyone will be accountable for his or her choices, has was always been a very important principle of Mormon doctrine.

Henry had to keep reminding himself that his life keep pace with the pressing responsibilities of parenthood. He was no longer in a partnership of raising five children to their fullest potentials. He struggled alone with the challenges of life, and he tended to the physical and emotional needs of his sons and daughters. He arose with the dawning of each new day and at night laid down in its vacuum of loneliness.

He fragmented himself five ways. Everything he did, he did for his children. Every decision he made, he made in their behalf: decisions regarding the business, the care of the children, and the best course to take for the future were his alone. He was afraid of the mistakes he would make. He had a lifetime to be afraid.

Laundry demanded immediate attention, the business had to be run, meals had to be cooked, the children needed attention, maintenance had to be done, diapers had to be changed, and bills had to be paid. Life had to go on without ceasing. Henry hired baby sitters and cleaning ladies for the times he needed them. Cousins who lived nearby came to his home on Sunday mornings to help get the children ready for Church. The support he had from everyone was unwavering. His friendships knew no bounds. He often received assistance from the ladies of the Relief Society, the women's auxiliary of the Church.

The rotation of the seasons closed its winter chapter on the desert town. The blooms of the cactus lilies on the distant horizon reminded Henry that changes must come about. Changes invited opportunities for experiences and adversity. Henry wondered if each new seasonal bloom of the cactus lilies would weaken the intensity of his despair. If they did, would there be any measure of guilt to replace the easement of his grief?

Occasionally Henry found himself smiling. At first, when he felt the joy of it he quickly and consciously replaced it with sorrow. He reminded himself that smiling was not within his boundaries. He struggled with the conflicts of emotions that came from losing his wife, soul-mate, and the mother to his five little children. He made necessary adjustments to his role in life. Through their actions, his children continually reminded him that he was left alone to nurture them. He did whatever was necessary for success. He was satisfied with the progress of his stewardship, but he was still concerned for the future.

The passing of time began to force the vision of Grace to slip further from him. In defense of his well-being, he began to accept the fact that his beloved was gone from his life until the time they would meet in the next phase of eternal progression. He knew he would always cherish the memories they had together, and knew he would forever feel the pain of his loss.

Springtime continued. The cactus lilies lost the blooms. The dry heat of the desert made the older children irritable. The boys were out of school for the summer.

The sound of a knock at the front door sent Henry cautiously and hesitantly toward it. It wasn't a familiar knock. He had learned to recognize the different densities of the knocking sounds made by those who came to visit. He opened the door to see a man and a woman from a social service agency. Henry invited his visitors to come into his home. He tried to make them feel at ease. Likewise they tried to make him feel at ease. It wasn't easy because of what they were about to say.

"Mr. Clayland, you are in a situation here that isn't typical for healthy family living. You, alone, are trying to be responsible for a large family of very young children. This is not beneficial to your children."

Henry was stunned at what was being said to him. The accusations in their voices, as if he wasn't worthy to be a father to his own children! He wanted to tell them to just leave, go away and leave him and his family alone.

The social workers looked around the room as though it was contaminated. "You are neither capable nor qualified of raising such young children. This is not natural, and it's not normal. Every one of these children need to have better living conditions than this."

Henry wouldn't let them get the best of him. Just because the laundry was piling up on the sofa it didn't mean that their home was dysfunctional.

"My family is well and thriving. I take care of my children. I give them what they need. Right now they need each other. Their mother isn't with us, but I manage on my own."

"Your children need the nurturing influence of a woman in their home. Our job is to see that neglected children are taken out of their current situation and placed in a home where they can thrive. It will be necessary for us to put your children in foster care until you resolve this issue. It's the best thing to do for you and your children. You will be receiving a court order to have the children taken from you if you don't do something soon, very soon."

Henry felt devastated and verbally assaulted. He could never allow his children to be put into foster care. The enormous task of raising children was difficult. Never in his life had he been more challenged, more humbled and so tired. Two strangers stood before him telling him what they thought he wasn't capable of. They knew nothing about him and what he was going through. He felt alarmed at the thought of his children being separated from him and from each other but he maintained his composure. He needed to keep his children together. They needed each other. Separating his family would be an act of betrayal. He was no psychologist, but he didn't need to be a psychologist to understand his own children and what their needs were.

He had to come up with a quick defense, one that was buried deep inside of him, reluctant to surface. "I have relatives that are willing to take them."

After Grace died, when his grief was so intense that he wasn't able to function coherently, he had thought of turning to his extended family. His and Grace's parents, his brothers and sisters, Grace's brothers and sisters, and a cousin or two offered to take the children into their homes. He appreciated their concerns and their offers but declined them. The children that God gave him were his responsibility. Most of all, they needed to be together as an immediate family.

He was intimidated into going against this judgment that he had formed from everything about him: his life with Grace, his family, his religion, and his subculture intermingled with his life's experiences. Why he allowed the intimidation to get the best of him, he didn't know. Perhaps it was because they were minutely right. He began to make accusations against himself. Perhaps he wasn't such a good single parent after all.

He shut a door behind him.

Henry was determined that the separation from his children would only be for a short while. He made that promise to them. Henry took the two older boys to live with him in Greer Arizona where he worked as a laborer in a saw mill. After paying off the legal fees and mortgage on the hotel, Henry wasn't left with a lot of money to get a new start. They ended up living in a shabby little rental shack with no running water and no indoor plumbing. The other children were left with relatives: Derek with our mother's parents, and Carl, Annabelle, and me with our father's parents. Grace's parents had relocated to their home in Anaheim after spending a year in New York where they had been doing service for the Mormon Church. The purpose of their move was to be there for Henry if he needed them.

Annabelle and Carl enjoyed playing in the wide and open spaces of the fresh Arizona terrain where the grandparents lived. Grandma and Grandpa affectionately doted upon all three of us. Seventy-year old Grandmother had the responsibility of caring for three little children while taking care of her ailing husband. Because he was terminally ill with cancer, Grandfather was confined to a wheelchair. Grandfather had the responsibility of bottle-feeding me. When I learned to crawl I would pull myself onto Grandfather's lap, lay my ear against his chest and listen to the rhythm of his beating heart while he fed me from my baby bottles. My heart was turned to his heart, and his to mine.

Grandfather watched me crawl around on the screened porch at their home while he sat in his wheelchair. Once he saw me pick up a stinkbug and treat it as though it was a gourmet delicacy. He didn't have a chance to retrieve the insect in time. After the incident, he was relieved of some of his duties.

Henry went searching for a wife. He was feeling the pressure from those who felt they knew what was best for him and his children. He was no longer running a home-based business. He was unsuccessful at collecting social security benefits that would cover the cost of a nanny and homemaker. He needed a woman in his home on a full-time and permanent basis. The fact was dictated so by the expectations of society and the social system within it. The children needed to be together and stay together at all costs. He needed to do whatever it took to make it so. He didn't want his well-intended relatives to have reason to put pressure on him. But finding someone interested in marrying a widowed man with five young children wasn't an easy task.

Jensine was a young woman of thirty years when she became acquainted with Grace's parents. She was an attractive woman ten years younger than Henry. Her long, soft, copper-red hair and hazel eyes were distinctly different from Grace's dark brown curly hair and dark blue eyes. Jensine's father was an emigrant from Denmark who had come to America with his parents when he was but a child. Her mother was born and raised in the Utah settlement, Logan. It was through the acquaintance with Grace's mother and father that she met Henry. They began their relationship by communicating through the mail. Henry told her right away that he had five motherless children; and he informed her of their ages, and he sent her a picture of them. When she saw the photograph of the five little orphans, Jensine found a spot for them inside her tender heart. She and Henry talked of a future together.

Jensine's parents were concerned when they learned that their daughter would be instantly endowed with a family of five children with a deceased mother, but they were grateful their daughter was able to fulfill a goal in her life. Though they questioned the motives of their future son-in-law at first, they gave the couple their blessing. Close to one year after Grace's death, Jensine became Henry's new wife and stepmother to his five children. They married in the Mormon Temple where "until death do you part" is not included in the marriage vows. Marriage in the "House of the Lord" extended into the afterlife. They were joined in the bonds of eternal marriage just as Grace and Henry had been.

One week after the wedding Grandfather was relieved of his pain and suffering. Although my temporal bond with him became broken, my eternal bond with him remained intact.

Four

Henry gathered his five children together, hoping to settle into a stable life raising them with the assistance of Jensine. The family settled in Burbank, California. Henry became the family's sole supporter from the income he received from his welding job at an aircraft manufacturing plant.

The home they bought was a small stucco and clapboard bungalow situated on a corner lot. The front door opened into a plank-floored living room. An adjacent dining room was wallpapered with robins perched on tree branches blossoming with pink flowers. It was the only room in the house that felt mellow. A kitchen of speckled counter-tops led to a laundry room that offered the use of a door leading to the back yard. A large flagstone patio began at the laundry room door and ended at the detached garage. The living room had a fireplace that was never used because of Jensine's fear of fire. A decorative carving of a genie lantern adorned the mantle. The children imagined that the genie lantern was a candy dish that offered many delightful candies at our every whim: peppermint, butterscotch, and chocolate drops were the favorites. The rest of the house consisted of two bedrooms and one bathroom. A den was converted to a bedroom where all the brothers slept.

The one-car garage held the artifacts that Henry had acquired in South Africa when he was a missionary. The usual collection of lawn and garden tools, along with life-long treasures, also remained safe in the garage where the children were not allowed to play. Henry had an interest in photography and its subjects so he built a darkroom in the far corner of the garage to pursue his interest in film development. He developed the negative of his five little children who were once labeled motherless and he made several prints from it. Among his collection of photographs he developed was the photo of Serenity that Grace had taken at the time when his life was serene. He kept the photograph, an imaged history of him and time, stored in a shoe-box, tucked into the darkness of fond memories that were too painful to bring into the light.

Jensine assumed the role of housekeeper and mother to Henry's children. She hoped and prayed that she would successfully bond with them. She understood that breaking ties to their biological mother would be difficult. She was determined to become as patient and affectionate with Grace's children as they allowed her to be.

Henry's love for Jensine was out of respect and admiration. He was grateful to her for her willingness to be a helpmate to him under such difficult circumstances. But the love from his past haunted him, and grief still weighed heavily on him. Whenever he looked at his growing children, he was reminded of Grace's contribution to his fatherhood. He wasn't able to forget Grace. He wasn't sure that he wanted to forget her.

In providing for his family, Henry was fraudulent in the affairs of the heart. He married Jensine in his state of desperation. In the unselfish act of sacrifice that was required to keep his family together, he brought a new trial into his already turbulent life. For his extended family members the action was admirable. For his new bride the action was insufferable. He judged himself harshly for what he had done. He struggled with the conflicts within him and justified his guilt by asking himself if he'd had any other choice. He lived a paradox of deception. He argued with his controversy. He thought he was being successful at nurturing his children after their mother died. It was difficult to play the role of both father and mother to five little children. He only wanted to keep the children together and be their father. He hoped that as time advanced away from the memories of Grace, the terrible injustice he had inflicted upon Jensine would somehow correct itself.

When Jensine first met Henry, she could sense his desperation. When she saw the pictures of his children, she wanted to be part of their lives. Henry seemed to be a responsible person, and his strength impressed her. She accepted his proposal of marriage and hoped that their union would be a union of maturing love and companionship. She was determined to be an ideal stepmother. But within her marriage, she felt as though she was living in the shadows of a love never to be forgotten. It wasn't long before Jensine was able to sense Henry's underlying motive for marriage. She began to feel used, unloved, and unappreciated.

Aside from the issues of the heart, Jensine's belly began to swell. The family grew, and the children grew.

Five

Plants and flowers surrounded the house and brought a variety of interesting colors to the intersection. A rose bed landscaped into the corner of the front yard was filled with a variety of colorful strains. Henry planted trees far enough away from the bed to allow enough sunshine for the roses. He planted trees, one representing each of his children, and he taught each child how to take care of it. The yard filled quickly with trees.

They planted a little vegetable garden in the back yard near the brick wall that separated their yard from the neighbor's. The little vegetable garden was situated against the fence to allow room for plants and flowers. Marigolds grew adjacent to the garden, snapdragons grew near the marigolds, zinnias grew near the snapdragons, pansies grew near the zinnias, and they planted a patch of dichondra nearby just to see if it would grow as well.

In the evenings, Jensine watered all of it except for the evidences of Bermuda grass: a wild and obnoxious variety that was most unwelcome because of its strangling attributes. She would cling to her garden hose possessively, as though it were a privilege and an honor to water the grass. The life-giving water flowing from the garden hose mesmerized her into reflecting moments. It was total peace and a distraction from the usual sorrow that beset her. She liked the fresh air and the chance to get out of the house for a while.

During the day, when she was inside taking care of the cleaning and the nurturing, she sent the older children outside to play. It made the house much less crowded. It was a good yard to play in. The climate was typically good because it was Southern California. It was a decade when the sky was almost always blue, and the clouds could get wonderfully imaginative.

Henry went daily to his blue-collar job by catching a car pool at a busy intersection a half-mile from home. He walked to his car pool, although he could have driven the family automobile. Within the ten-year span of Burbank residency, Henry owned a Ford pickup, a Hudson, a Chevy Bel-Air, and a Studebaker. Each vehicle was almost new when he bought it. Jensine refused to drive. Learning to drive was another one of her fears. The family vehicle stayed parked in the driveway until Henry got behind the wheel to drive it to the essential places: Church and the market places. If the kids wanted to go anywhere else they had to walk to get there.

Jensine learned to tolerate her demented marriage with its five appendages. She learned early on that some of Henry's children were not as sweet as they appeared in the photograph that Henry had mailed to her. She feared her commitments under the circumstances, but felt that love, patience, and understanding would overcome the obstacles. No one had forced her to accept Henry's proposal. She thought that romantic love had begun and that love would continue to grow. She thought she did the right thing by marrying Henry. She thought the Lord would have been pleased with her act of unselfishness.

She became determined to exist within her deprivations, and she took her commitments seriously. She sought to achieve her goals. She brought into the world her own children who would love her, and she would return their love. Having these children gave comfort to her anguish. The more children she had, the more love she felt. She announced to the family that it was time to cease bringing little spirits into the world when a delivery-room nurse informed her that Henry fell asleep in the father's waiting room as she labored to give birth to her fourth child, his ninth.

Jensine directed her life within the boundaries of her religion. She was determined to keep her actions within the doctrines of the Church. The times when she packed her bags and gathered her children to return to her Utah homeland were the few times she almost failed. Her parents had died since the time of the wedding, and her siblings had lives of their own. It wasn't sensible to permanently stay with her siblings. Just as there was no option for Henry, there was no option for Jensine. To stay joined was their destiny and their duty. Their obligation of parenthood was the driving force in their lives. Each had to live within their dominions of despair and deal with it.

Throughout our lives Carl, Annabelle, Derek, Tom and I never called Jensine by any name other than "Mamma." We thought that to call Jensine "Mother" was to betray the mother we were born to because the name was too linked with lineage. "Mom" seemed to be reserved for her own children that she gave birth to. To call her "Jensine" wasn't appropriate for a matriarch in a family who assisted in the nurturing of her husband's children.

Shortly after the wedding my stepmother Jensine and I began a warm and affectionate relationship with each other. In the early years of being part of Jensine's life, Carl and I often climbed upon her lap and listened to stories she read from a storybook. There was softness, warmth, and tenderness, but slowly someone else began to demand our loyalty. Our loyalty was for a mother we could never see, never talk to, never feel, and never touch; a mother we could only imagine. Carl seemed to be able to mitigate his loyalties better than I did.

Derek enjoyed making kites and flying them. He became the neighborhood adviser for how to build them and make them soar high in the sky. He made the kite tails out of anything he could get his hands on. My old and faded dress, much too worn out to pass on to anyone else, made an impressively long kite tail when shredded and tied just right.

Derek commanded the kite into the air by running down the middle of the street, carefully avoiding the telephone wires. He deviated from his course only at the approach of automobiles. The kite caught a shaft of wind and the wind took over the lift as he released the string. The street-sponsored baseball game that operated almost daily in the television-deprived neighborhood came to a halt. The curious participants drew their attention to the kite high in the air. My big brother could do anything!

My faded flowered dress floated, a long tail flapping in the wind. I was glad the old worn dress could be converted to such an important product. It was the dress that I got wet one day in an attempt to help Mamma. I wanted to wash the dress so that Mamma wouldn't have to. It seemed that Mamma was always bending over the tub of the ringer washer and running the wet clothing though the rollers of the ringer. My soiled dress was one less thing for Mamma to wash.

In a state of enthusiasm I entered the bathroom. I examined my face in the mirror and I liked what I saw. I was about to initiate a new way in which Americans could wash their laundry. I took a washcloth and soaked it in water and then proceeded to wash my dress while I was still wearing it. *Why take off my dress?* I asked myself. I rubbed the water from the washcloth deep into the fabric to get out anything that was deviant. I covered the front of the dress with wetness. The wetness darkened the faded splotches of fabric.

"Mamma will be so proud of me, and she'll be happy that I am so clever." I felt very innovative, creative, and I was helping Mamma as well. There were a lot of children in the family. Mamma had plenty to do. I finished my self-inflicted assignment.

Because the day was warm, I knew I needed to find Mamma quickly before the air changed my dress back into its faded flowers. I opened the bathroom door and followed the sounds coming from the laundry room. The sounds from the washer always brought Mamma into focus: a stepmother bent over the wringer washing tub shoving drenched clothes through the rolling wringers. Sometimes Mamma would let me run the clothes through the ringer, but she seemed worried that I would catch my little fingers in the cylinder rollers.

I felt happy to be approaching Mamma. It wasn't very often that I had an opportunity to make Mamma happy. "Mamma, look! I washed my dress all by myself."

I couldn't wait to feel Mamma's approval. I was wrong about Mamma being happy. Mamma always had to do things the standard way. Also, it seemed impossible for Mamma to be happy about anything.

Derek often reminded me that Mamma wasn't my real mother. He told me about my real mother and explained to me that she was an angel in heaven. He told me that she would be seeing me from time to time but I wouldn't be able to see her, and that our real mother had her own special way of taking care of us. Derek was six years older than me. He knew everything. My mother was my guardian angel! The beautiful angel roamed around in a state of obscurity, wanting to take care of things that should be taken care of but not being able to, only able to watch and wish that she could. She wanted to embrace her children and bequeath them with her love. My angel mother knew things about me that my stepmother didn't. The angel was half of me, she looked more like me than the Mamma that was inside the house doing the daily things of mammas that had skin you could touch.

Derek took his dreams to heart. The stories you didn't put in your head had to come from somewhere. What better place than from up there? At least grasp on to the good ones, the ones worthwhile, and ones you can allow for determination of destiny. It was okay to discard the bad ones, the ones that were no good for you. Derek's definition of dreams had been established at a very young and tender age. His mother told him of her dreams of having many children, a message to her from above. His mother's death, then her status as angel, influenced his thoughts and his attitudes.

Derek became concerned with the affairs of immortality. He often pondered the mysteries of God's kingdom. Derek often looked at the sky, and in the nighttime he looked towards Kolob: the place where God dwelled. He used to lie on the grass under the massive assortment of stars and planets and wonder which shiny planet in the universe was Kolob.

The stepmother in Derek's life was the obstacle in his path of progression. He determined that it was she who was to be his life's greatest nemesis; after all, she took his mother's place in the home they were supposed to call functional. She was always in the kitchen cooking her Danish recipes, she washed clothes his mother was supposed to wash, she swept the floor with a broom that belonged to his mother, and she slept in the bed his mother was supposed to sleep in. Worst of all, she took the liberty of telling his siblings what they should do, and what they shouldn't do. That was his league, his territory, and his duty. Mother said it to him in her room. Her voice faded as Dad carried her away from them. "Take care of your brothers and sisters." He never forgot it, and he never would.

"Jensine, you will never be my mother." He mostly said it to himself, but he said it to Jensine on the occasions when the statement was called for. No woman could ever love him like his own mother did. Derek felt he failed in the duty that his mother had last requested. He didn't understand himself. And he didn't understand why things couldn't be the way they were supposed to be.

Tom was a young teenager when his father married again. He thought of his mother often, and he missed the long talks they had. The year after her death he often thought about the time he last saw her, and he remembered the words she said to him. He did take care of his brothers and sisters, but he wasn't going to make a career out of it. He was there for them. They had a special bond. When he saw his mother for the last time, he expected her to return to them. She went to the hospital to get better, not to die. Then he decided to let go of her. It was too hard to hold on to her when he had so much to live for.

Annabelle was insecure, confused, and unsure of herself. She missed her mother, though the memories of her were very dim. The most vivid memories were of the funeral. Her father lifted her to the casket so she could see her mother one last time. Her mother was lying motionless upon a shiny sheet, unable to embrace her. Annabelle remembered a lid coming down, shutting her mother inside an abyss of terrifying blackness. She wasn't able to comprehend it. No one could explain it coherently. Her mother went to live with Heavenly Father! Why would her mother leave when she needed her? She remembered wailing for her mother at the gravesite. She remembered the hole in the ground and the casket positioned above it. The hole was dark and ready to steal. She could hear and feel her heart pulsate aggressively inside her chest. No one had to tell her that her mother was going to be lowered into the earth. She reasoned it on her own. Someone picked her up and held her. She couldn't remember who it was. She did not feel comforted.

Carl was always tenderhearted and dear. He got confusing messages all through his early years. He took the tensions that lingered at home in stride.

I had been told at a very young age that my mother died when I was a baby. My father talked about her one day on the way to Church when Jensine wasn't with us. At the time, I thought that I wasn't any different than anyone else. I thought that everyone had a different mother than the one they were born to. I thought that everyone had a dead mother. It was probably at a time when I was confused about many things.

My father rarely spoke of Mother Grace. As a small child it didn't cross my mind that my father and my real mother had domestic experience with each other. As I grew the concept of "mother" reassembled. I made up stories about a real mother and father and I allowed my imagination to soar. There were stories about the seven of us being together as a family doing the things that real families do. We laughed together, had dinner together and got tucked into bed at night by a father and a mother who were real. I was supposed to be able to call someone "Mother" but I never had the honor of it. I knew for certain that Jensine would never hear the word "Mother" from me. My father betrayed me by giving me a stepmother: a false mother.

It was sad to hear stories about my mother. At the same time it was sad not to hear them. Would my whole life be enveloped in sadness? Perhaps it was why my father relied heavily on other people to tell Annabelle, my brothers, and me about our mother. He approached Grace's cousins she grew up with, her brothers and sisters, and anyone he knew who had memorable experiences. He requested that stories be written about her, documented upon paper to be preserved for his posterity so they could become superficially acquainted with the matriarch of his eternal family. He wrote a diary of major events in their lives together. The statue Serenity was mentioned. The courtship at the feet of Serenity was recorded in his journal and in his diary. He saved letters that Grace had written. He gave the stories, letters, and accounts to his and Grace's children.

I was told the stories as though stories were all that I deserved. But for them to remain unrecorded was cruel and unfair to my heritage. The words were like the fantasies I kept inside my mind, fantasies that any motherless child would harbor. I had a fantasy of being inside a womb that once existed. I envied other children from the moment I learned that babies grew inside mothers. *They glance at their bellies and they think to themselves, "I used to be in there."* To them it wasn't a fantasy. My mother had become my secret. The stories always remained silent, held inside, unqualified to be revealed. My mother lived inside a journal too painful to open.

Inside my brothers' bedroom I stared at the framed portrait of the lady who was supposed to be taking care of me, feeding me, teaching me, and wiping away my tears. She was pretty. Her hair was straight and laid flat on top. Sparkling hair clips that pressed on her temples allowed swirls of wavy curls to accent the oval shape of her face. I wondered if my mother's hair had been permed or if it was natural. My mother always looked the same in the photograph, her chin was always tilted the same, and her face was always tinted in a soft tone of brown, and I could imagine the dark blue eyes that were envied by all her cousins.

In art class at school, I made a Mother's Day card. I pretended I was going to give it to my real mother. I decorated my card with red paper hearts that I cut from construction paper. I wrote a poem on the card copied from the blackboard. With the card in my hand, I began my walk home from school. As I got closer to home, my mother's blue eyes mutated back to brown in my mind, becoming the color that the photo dictated. Just a framed photograph would be there as it always was. Jensine was the flesh and the blood. Then I ripped the card into small pieces and fed it to the storm drain. I sat on the curb, laid my face in my hands, and pouted. When I got home, I didn't go into my brothers' room. I was angry at my real mother for dying. I wondered if she knew it.

At the acquisition of a television the children became patrons of "The Mickey Mouse Club" and daily followed the "Adventures of Spin and Marty." The only exception was each Tuesday, the day the kids in the family walked the three-mile round trip to attend Primary: the Church's auxiliary for children. The Clayland family attended Church regularly and devoutly.

Throughout my childhood, I listened intently as the doctrines of the Church were being expounded. I caught on quickly to the ones that applied to my life. The doctrine of the sealing powers, or the eternal bonding of families, became the most significant to me. It was taught that, in the perspective of eternity, mortality was only a minute part of one's span of existence. The time would come when my spirit would leave my body and press on to the next stage of progression, and I would come face to face with my mother. I wondered what kind of a rapport my mother and I would have.

My mother didn't have the opportunity of raising her children to maturity, and her children didn't have the opportunity of being raised to maturity by their mother. I wondered if we would have a mother and child relationship. Would Tom, Derek, Annabelle, and Carl pick up from where they left off? Would our mother insist on fulfilling her promise she had made to them in that December of long ago? She promised her children that they would make candy, popcorn balls, and pretty butterflies together. Would there be a way to do it in heaven? And would we celebrate Christmas together? Or would everyone become adult friends together in a spiritual heaven and talk about only the adult things that apply to issues not of mortality?

For the many years in Burbank, Henry buried his turmoil in what the Church terms the Spirit of Elijah: genealogical research. He mailed requests for birth records, census records, marriage records, and death records to submit his ancestors' names to the temples for the purpose of having religious ordinance work done vicariously for them.

Grace and Henry were descendants of the early Mormon settlers of the west. Their people were among the refugees of religious persecution who escaped their enemies by fleeing to the virgin western territories of the American continent. Their people were among those who saw a barren desert and a chance to turn it into a fertile and fruitful valley. They were among those who made the desert "blossom as a rose." The desert that blossomed as a rose became the Great Salt Lake Valley and the settlements along the Wasatch Front.

The first Mormon missionaries assigned to Denmark converted Grace's maternal ancestors to the religion. Putting aside their fears for the unknown, her grandparents joined the main body of Mormons in America in 1855 and became pioneers to Zion, where the "pure in heart" dwelled. They relied upon God and each other. There never was a better opportunity to display their courage and faith.

The pioneers accepted whatever fates befell them. They were already well acquainted with suffering and death. They expected it to happen to them. *And should we die before our journey's through, happy day, all is well*: the psalm of faith and courage became their music. They sought a permanent home, far from the government that refused to protect them from malicious and murderous mobs, far from the governor of Missouri who had ordered their executions and expulsions. During the arduous journey, three of Grace's ancestors and two of Henry's died on the prairie pushing handcarts. Either starvation or disease took them.

Brigham Young was the chosen spiritual and political leader of the settlers. They looked to him for strength amid uncertainty. The adversities they suffered in the east were still fresh in their memories. Brigham was a god-fearing man who strongly warned the saints to shun pride and remain humble. He promised blessings to those who did. Brigham Young assigned families to colonize the territories throughout the west: Utah, Arizona, Nevada, Idaho, Colorado, and New Mexico. The settlers willingly looked to new horizons and new opportunities. Brigham Young went down in American history as one of the great colonizers of America. Families mingled and married. They felt fortunate to be a contributor to the building of Zion and her stakes.

Grace's pioneer family was assigned to St Johns, Arizona. Henry's pioneer families moved south into New Mexico after they established Pond Town, Utah, later renamed Salem after Lyman Curtis's land of heritage: Salem, Massachusetts.

Lyman Curtis, Henry's great-grandfather, was with the company of pioneers who first entered the Salt Lake Valley. He accompanied Brigham Young, leader of the exodus, as they entered the valley at Emigration Canyon. With the Wasatch Front behind them, they faced a challenging panorama before them. The vision was with Brigham Young. The prophet swept his hand across the salty flat of the valley and proclaimed, "It is enough; this is the right place, drive on." Lyman watched a handful of men prepare the soil on the valley floor for harvest before winter. Shadrack Roundy, one of those plowing the desert soil, became a great-great grandfather to Grace.

Through family research, Henry and Grace Clayland learned that they were descendants of the early Mormon polygamists. Until the year 1880 polygamy, the marriage of a man to more than one wife, was practiced among select Mormon men. Many single pioneer women needed to attach to a man for financial, social, and emotional support, and for the continuance of the human race. According to the Mormon faith, plural marriage was sanctioned by the doctrines of the Church under divine inspiration. It was newly manifested in religious context. The Church complied with a federal law that was eventually initiated against it. So Wilford Woodruff, the prophet and president of the Church at the time, and a successor of Brigham Young, received a revelation to abolish polygamy. The Lord desired that the doctrines of the Church be compatible with the laws of the land.

Henry hoped that his deceased ancestors in the generations beyond the pioneers accepted the ordinances from the knowledge that they might acquire in their post-mortal life. Baptisms, endowments, and sealings of families to each other-ordinances performed only for mortal beings-were done by proxy for his kindred dead to allow them into his religion. The free will of man continued to be respected even beyond the veil. It was the choice of the deceased to accept or reject the ordinances. Henry had become the family research representative for the Clayland extended family.

In the ten years of living in Burbank, the Clayland family progressed within their sphere of functionality. Discord continued and intensified with each passing year. Jensine's unhappiness intensified as well. She continued to feel used and unloved. Her own children softened her sorrow and made her unhappiness tolerable. She bonded with them as a natural mother would.

"Wicked Stepmother Syndrome" plagued the family like a cancer. Throughout the years Derek continued to vocalize his feelings regarding Stepmother Jensine. He always made her understand that he wouldn't, under any circumstances, ever accept her. He defied her authority, and he was continuously belligerent towards her. His opinions and his actions didn't set a good example for his brothers and sisters. He continued to take his brotherly duties seriously, and he felt as though he must protect and defend his siblings. He would never forget the last words of his dying mother: "Take care of your brothers and sisters."

A division was felt between the two sets of Henry's children. There were the little kids (Jensine's), and there were the big kids (Grace's). It became a standard in the Clayland household. A father was the only thing the two groups had in common.

Two weeks short of Henry's tenth anniversary of working for the aircraft company, and two weeks before he was eligible to draw full pension benefits, the company laid him off.

Six

Henry grew a moustache and called it his escrow moustache. None of the kids knew what the word escrow meant. He told them he would leave the moustache on his upper lip until the time the house sold. After it sold, Henry and Jensine made a down payment on a thirty-five acre raisin farm in the middle of the San Joaquin Valley, the "Raisin Capitol of the World".

The San Joaquin Valley, the stretch of fertile land that reached from Sacramento to Bakersfield, was the chance for Henry to continue with the stewardship to feed, shelter, and clothe the eight children who were still under his wing. Fresno, located in the middle of the valley, had scorching temperatures in the summers and freezing temperatures in the winters. Snowfall was unheard of, and the chance of rainfall in the summers was not typical. The snowfall from the Sierra Nevada mountain range, east of the valley, provided irrigation water to the farms of the valley. Alfalfa, cotton, olives, grapes, tomatoes, and fruits of all kinds grew abundantly in the sandy and fertile soil. The vast, flat terrain in the summer was ideal for the production of raisins. There never was a more labor-intensive crop.

Henry got a good deal on a farm of Thompson seedless grapes. If raisin production didn't earn a good profit there wouldn't have been so many raisin farms in the valley, he reasoned. He didn't think he would be involved in any more labor than any other raisin farmer. Henry liked the idea of being a farmer. He was no longer a young man. He was in his early fifties. He weighed the advantages of farming: he would be able to work at his own pace, and he had sons and daughters who could help with the crops. Twelve miles southwest of the city of Fresno, the family began the transition from one style of living to another.

The farm was desolate, a drastic change from the urban neighborhood of Burbank that spilled noisy and lively children onto the streets. A chain of life challenges was in the forecast for the Clayland family. The year was 1958. Tom was on his mission for the Church in Peru. Derek was in the middle of his high school years, and Annabelle was beginning it. Carl, David, Annette, Diana and I rode the school bus together to the closest elementary school. Spencer wasn't in school yet.

The small farmhouse, barn, chicken coop, propane tank, tool house, and outhouse were situated upon three acres off Grapevine Drive. The house was very old and had obviously been built without the restraints of building codes. The plumbing lines were of unusual design and dimension. We always had to flush the toilet with a bucket of water because it was impossible any other way. Whenever we flushed, we could watch the sewage make its way to the septic tank by peering into the drain hole of the bathtub. We knew how to do it slowly and skillfully enough so that the dirty toilet water wouldn't come up into the bathtub. Everyone got quite skilled with the flushing technique. However, the bathroom had a lingering bad odor that no amount of cleaning was able to dispel.

Uncle Samuel, Grace's youngest brother, was a doctor like Edwin. He and his wife, Mari, lived in the foothills with his large family of immaculate children. Uncle Samuel occasionally came out to the farm and checked on the family whenever we got sick. He prescribed medicine when necessary. No one in the family got sick very often. We were attacked by boils more often than any other ailment. Uncle Samuel taught the family how to avoid them but they continued to be a menace. After doing family practice for several years, Uncle Samuel decided to specialize in ophthalmology. He went through the necessary training and became a very prominent eye surgeon for Central California, taking patients in from the northern and southern parts of the state.

Aunt Hannah, one of Grace's sisters, also lived in Clovis, a town near Fresno. She and her family lived in a two-bathroom house with toilets that had incredible flushing capabilities. The big kids from our family loved to go to her house and play with the cousins. A railroad track beyond their back fence was close enough for the kids to wave at all the passing trains. One day, Aunt Hannah and her husband Uncle Joe went on a business trip to Southern California. The trip became the final chapter of her life on earth when an intoxicated truck driver killed her in a traffic accident. Aunt Hannah was the same age as Grace when she died. She also left behind five young children, only slightly older than Grace's had been.

Aunt Ellen was another one of Grace's sisters who also lived near Fresno. She and her family lived on an affluent side of town. While there, she became the author of a national best seller.

The Clayland house had a large kitchen in relation to the rest of the house. It enabled the shabby Formica dinette set to be placed there, shoved close to a wall. When having meals together, the skinniest kids in the family were assigned to the chairs against the wall. Jensine was delighted with the kitchen range, which looked very new and modern. It had a grill built right in the middle of it. The big kids determined that the modern range was the only reason Mamma and Daddy must have bought the house, the property, and everything that it entailed. The modern kitchen range was the cause of our despair. If the farmhouse at the orange orchard had a modern kitchen range, one of the farms that Mamma and Daddy looked at when they went shopping for property, then we would all be picking oranges instead of picking grapes that we had to turn into raisins.

The house had two bedrooms and a small closed-in front porch that was converted into a bedroom for a boy or two. It was tricky trying to figure out where to put eight dependents. Annabelle and I slept in a little room without a closet. Too many drafty windows made the room very cold in the winters. A couple of other girls slept on beds in an alcove near the bathroom that always smelled bad.

The shed that was located about ten yards from the house was converted into a bedroom for the older boys. It contained a propane heater, as though the shed had originally been intended to be living quarters for a migrant family. The shed had a shoddy closet that mice attacked and two windows that brought in dusty sunlight. A tall wooden dresser had Carl's name scratched across the front of it. Jensine always assumed that he was the one that did the autographing, but it was I who did the defacing. I thought it was more fun and much easier to write Carl's name than it was my own. Sweet and dear Carl never bothered to correct the misunderstanding and took the blame without complaint. On the east-side of the room, Henry kept his desk and his file cabinets to maintain his genealogical research, although it had waned. Tracked-in sand lingered everywhere, etching swirly patterns into the cheap linoleum floor and stripping color off in significant areas. At the outside corner of the shed, a patch of Bermuda grass bullied its way through a crack in the floor and acted as if no one had any say in the matter.

The barn located beyond the boys' room was large and unpainted. I didn't like to go inside because it was dark, even with the rays of light squeezing through the cracks between the slats. The walls of the barn looked frightening with the strange-looking tools hanging on them. The only time I went inside the barn was to marvel at the puppies that Lucky, the family dog, gave birth to. A stranger came by the house one day and made an offer to purchase boards from the barn. He wanted them to make a plank floor for his home. Henry sold enough from the back of the barn to satisfy them both. The transaction made the barn become a subtle eyesore to any motorist who traveled the road behind the barn. Because the missing planks brought in plenty of natural sunlight, I was able to go into the stripped middle section of the barn without being afraid.

A cow on the property provided creamy milk daily. The boys milked her and put her out to pasture. The little kids had fun watching a small goldfish grow to a large size in the cow's drinking trough. No one bothered to feed the goldfish. We determined that it ate the stuff that fell off the cow. The cow trough was near the gas pump. The gas tank was kept filled for the operation of the tractor, and the family car was fed.

Jensine's green thumb made the outside of the house look nice. She planted some of her favorite plants and flowers. The flowers reminded the kids of their former neighborhood in Burbank. She watered the plants with the same mannerisms and devoutness that she had in Burbank. She hung onto her garden hose possessively and devoutly, and tenderly directed the water path onto the base of the plants. Watering her plants continued to be a spiritual experience for her, just as it was in Burbank.

Daddy planted fruit trees on the half-acre frontage between the highway and the house. Mature apricot trees that the birds went crazy over in the summer shielded the view of the home site from the section of the vineyard that pointed towards town.

Junk cars accumulated throughout the years. They were shoved in the back and abandoned behind the barn. Henry hoped that, one day, someone could fix them and they would run again. He wasn't the best at maintaining cars. He took care of only what was broken. When the brakes went out on the Studebaker station wagon, he resorted to the hand brake whenever he needed to stop the car as it moved down the long stretches of country roads. A charity repair job, a new junk car, or getting by with the worn-out vehicles became the solution for transportation. Money was always tight because something usually went wrong with the crops.

Raisins were made in the sun, as they had been historically. If disease or insect infestation didn't ruin them then rain at the wrong time did. Even more so than the nemeses of nature, surplus crops from the previous year brought on financial ruin for many of the small farmers. Before taking on more raisins, the buyers preferred that the previous year's raisins were sold. It eventually became necessary for acre upon acre of grape vineyards to convert to wine grapes. The wineries often had more offers than they could handle. Fruit flies went crazy over the unpicked grapes that fervently fermented upon the vines.

The family pruned and wrapped the selected branches around the heavy gauge wires that stretched down the rows. Wrapping the new vines on the wire to give support to the fruit was necessary to the procedure. If not handled skillfully, a branch would often hurl at the pruner and then slap him or her in the face. I knew that the mean old branches laughed at me every time they slapped me.

Migrant farm workers were usually hired to assist the family. The migrants were more available during the pruning season than during the harvest. The family did the weeding, the irrigation, and the preparation for the harvest. When it came time for the harvest, the farmers depended on the migrant Mexican farm workers. The migrants appeared to be poor and destitute but they seemed to be locked into happy families. The children, who the adults brought with them to labor, worked responsibly and cooperatively alongside their family members. The members of the families were devoted to each other, and the children seemed to be well adjusted within their itinerant life style.

If migrant workers were in short supply, the situation was serious. Too often this was the case. Grapes unable to be made into raisins due to labor shortage or the Cesar Chavez migrant worker strikes were converted to wine grapes or else they rotted on the vines. If the winery manufacturers were interested in buying the grapes, they offered to buy the crop for almost nothing, as if they were doing the farmer a favor to get the grapes off his hands.

The Thompson Seedless was intended for raisin production. If the crop didn't end up in the winepresses, the family and the hired workers worked together to pick the grapes for raisin production. After the grapes were picked, they were spread upon heavy paper trays that were laid upon level ground. The leveling of the ground was necessary to avoid mold from accumulating on the shrinking grapes if there happened to be precipitation. The teams picked the grapes and laid them on the trays, allowing the sun's rays to begin the conversion process.

After the picking was completed, the farmers typically paid the laborers in cash. Sometimes, if the previous year was good, Daddy would pay his kids for their work. With the fruit upon the ground, the family members humbled themselves to pray for compassion of the weather. Intensity of the sun furnished the time frame of production. The day came when the shrinking grapes had to be turned so that the sun could dry the other side of them. The fruit-filled paper trays were flipped onto clean ones to expose the plump side of the grapes once again. While the sun still lingered above, hopes were high that clouds wouldn't hinder its rays.

There was no machinery for the processing of the commodity, there was no relief for the spine. The teamwork of two laborers created a steady and synchronized horsepower. Knees in contact with the sandy earth, facing each other, the team turned the trays upside down onto a new sheet of paper: avoid spillage, be careful, keep your pace, and be responsible even if you're only eleven years old. If it weren't for the overalls and Cooley hats, one would think the grape turners were living in the same century as Jesus Christ.

The farmers were able to breathe more easily after the sun made its contribution. The paper trays of raisins still had to be folded, rolled, and strategically positioned on the ground to be picked up and loaded in the wagon that was pulled by the tractor.

After the harvest was gathered in, Henry made the kids put the raisins through the sifter to sift out sand and rocks that blew onto the trays as the grapes dried. Payment from the raisin buyers was made depending on weight. The other farmers didn't sift. Henry wanted to teach the kids to be honest. After the sifting was done, the raisins were packed in wooden crates that were stacked on top of each other near the pulley.

The property included five acres of clear land that was adjacent to a section of vineyard. Once, for one of his birthdays, Daddy bought a truckload of almond trees. We planted them on the vacant acreage. The almond trees flourished and sometimes provided bumper crops. The selling of almonds from these five acres was sometimes more profitable than selling the labor-intensive raisins from the thirty-five acres.

As the years went on, poverty continued at the Clayland homestead continued. Television, radio, and telephone service became nonexistent at times. If something broke, it stayed broken. There was no money to fix it or replace it. The little kids resorted to creating their own entertainment. They had to sit at the kitchen table, read library books, and draw and paint pictures in tablets of newsprint.

The day came when Henry had to let the vineyard succumb to the Bermuda grass and the weeds. His tidy vineyard collapsed. The upkeep of the enterprise was too intense and business wasn't profitable enough to hire help. It became necessary for him to take a job with the post office, working the rural routes near the farm. The thick Tulle fog that often rolled into the valley blinded the reason of the roads and sent motorists into frenzies. Henry decided it was just one more trial in his life he had to cope with. He also got a part-time job working with Del Monte as a raisin inspector, checking raisins to see if they were up to par before they went into the packages.

The chasm that had been generated in Burbank still persisted between the two sets of Henry's offspring. Carl remained cordial enough to be considered everyone's brother and friend. The big kids and the little kids continued to share a father but didn't share a mother. There were Henry's kids, and there were Jensine's kids.

For Christmas one year, Tom and Derek bought me and Annabelle a pink plastic electric radio. We were thrilled and excited to once again come into contact with civilization. We listened to the heartthrobs of the decade: Elvis, Buddy Holly, Bobby Vinton, Ricky Nelson, and others. We were swept up in the love ballads of Andy Williams and Nat King Cole. We gasped at the lyrics of the song, "Teen Angel." We wept together when Buddy Holly and his friends died in the plane crash.

The septic tank below the kitchen window that took in the kitchen's waste-water collapsed and became an open sewer. There was no money to replace it or fix it.

Jensine planted bushes and flowers around it to hide the evidence.

Henry developed deadly eating habits during the years at the farm. He acquired a taste for bread thoroughly soaked in bacon or beef grease. The viscous grease burgers became incorporated into his diet almost daily.

The marriage of Jensine and Henry was as it always was. Financial trials made Jensine feel stressed. She continued to feel unloved, unappreciated, and she suffered from depression, but she was determined to not abandon her marriage. Her stepchildren remained unconnected. As she relegated herself to a state of hopelessness, she lashed out in her bitterness. Each night she wept for the outcome of the choice she had made. Her own children were her strength and her motivation to not fall into hopeless despondency.

I became a recluse in my years at the farm. My unacceptable grades in school reflected the state of my emotions rather than my capabilities. I became withdrawn, secluded, and somewhat neurotic. I walked past the girls' restroom each day on the way to the school cafeteria to work the serving line so that I could earn my lunch. These were the days before entitlements. No one else was around, for everyone else was in the classrooms learning. It was a convenient time to go inside the restroom and raid the Kotex machine. I knew how to hit it just right so the contents would tumble out without putting a nickel in it. There wasn't any other way to get them, and I didn't dare tell Mamma that I needed them. It would be another reason for her to get stressed about. I justified my thievery by claiming the time and labor I spent sweating over the serving line in the school cafeteria was much more than what my lunch was worth. I could go on with more poverty and hardship stories.

Why couldn't Daddy have stayed at his hotel and raised us without the interference of the social system and the agencies that think they know everything? How different things might have been for us. The hotel apartment was small, but at least it had a flushing toilet. We'd had the support of our friends and our Church. Daddy had earned a reasonable income and he had owned property. I thought a lot about "what ifs." And so I asked the question: How can a social agency know what the long-term effects will be for a forced directive that they make? Perhaps I wouldn't have had such a miserable childhood if the social system had not perceived that a man isn't qualified to nurture his children.

The day came when Henry had to come to a resolution for correcting some of the conflicts in his home. He was no longer able to deal with me. He approached Edwin and Charlotte about taking me into their home for my high school years. The plan was approved. Annabelle was to go with me. She was finished with high school.

Seven

We had always been very comfortable with Uncle Edwin and Aunt Charlotte. As children the big kids spent whole summers staying with them in the family's one bathroom, three-bedroom house in San Diego. Uncle Edwin had a prosperous medical practice, although it wasn't evident from the house they lived in. Our four cousins had always been delightful and fun. On some of the summer days of our childhood Aunt Charlotte took all of us to the swimming pool at the local park. On other days she dropped us off at the local movie theater so we could watch the double-feature cowboy and Indian movies plus ten cartoons.

We appreciated Edwin and Charlotte's graciousness and their generosity. This time it was not summer vacation. They became my legal guardians for the next four years. Before we left home to live with Uncle Edwin and Aunt Charlotte our father told Annabelle and me that he was glad we came to live with him. It was something he told us often. The trip to San Diego became a turning point in both our lives.

During a year when the big kids remained at the Fresno farm, Uncle Edwin and Aunt Charlotte moved to a large picturesque house on Grand Avenue. Everyone referred to the house as Snow White's cottage. The large, sugar-brown, two story stucco house accented with contrasting trim and had looming chimneys on opposite sides of the house that enticed ivy vines to climb their way to the top. A heavy, arched front door complimented the latticed window panes. Aunt Charlotte hated to drape them, for draping would hide the beauty of the panes.

Unlike all the neighbors' houses, this house was set far back from the avenue. The interior of the house was as charming as the exterior. Ceramic tiled floors on the first level and pure wool carpets in the living room and den could have qualified the house for feature in a magazine of home design and decorating. A secret door in the walnut-paneled den contained Edwin's photography equipment. An annexed apartment that had a bedroom suspended in air directly above the driveway became the living space for my sister and me. An unlit secondary stairway, adjacent to the garage, reached up to the main part of the apartment that was located above the garage.

Uncle Edwin and Aunt Charlotte took the family to the family reunions, which were held every other year in the mountains in Arizona. The forestland that Grace's grandparents homesteaded in the 1880s remained in the possession of the family. A cookhouse, a recreation hall, cabins, and outhouses were built from the lumber of the old sawmill that they had owned and operated. The reunions at the homestead were a haven from the harsh realities of loss that Grace's children had suffered. The relatives that surrounded us on the two scheduled days in early July happened to be the same relatives who wrote down their memories of Grace: the aunts and uncles, and the brothers and sisters who loved her. We, Grace's children, felt the connection with our heritage that our mother so lovingly bestowed upon us. Our mother was the missing link in our immediate eternal family. We felt the reality of the connection. We relished the spirit of the bond.

Annabelle began attending the local city college and then a university for a year before she got married. My cousins and I went to the local high school. I went from being a poor farmer's daughter to suddenly being thrust into an affluent lifestyle where gardeners attended the landscaping and maids did the domestic chores. Uncle Edwin and Aunt Charlotte made it a project to assist Henry's children in any way they could. After all, Edwin was Grace's brother and Charlotte was Henry's sister. They shared their love and their resources with their nieces and nephews. They helped with emotionally and financially challenging times. Edwin and Charlotte were more generous than they should have been. Edwin would often think of his sister, her begging to get home so she could make popcorn balls, candy, and some kind of butterflies. It couldn't happen. All the while, I would think, Daddy, can't you just figure out how to solve the problems in your home; then again, maybe there wasn't a way.

I went to school dutifully but without vision. My grades were acceptable but I was socially incompetent. There was a good supply of great looking boys but they seemed to be so unreachable. The kind of girls that boys liked were ones that had flashing smiles and sparkling eyes, like Sherry and her friend Kate. They were both very pretty and popular with the boys. They experienced it all: the drill team, the cheer-leading squad, and homecoming courts. One year, the two of them ran for homecoming queen. Kate was crowned. A few years later I wondered if the guys would have favored Sherry if they had known that, in the future, she would become a famous model. I didn't know how to make my eyes sparkle like their eyes.

In the four years at the same high school, teachers and peers weaved their influence into my character. They all had their own twist on life, it seemed. Mr. Francisco, the Spanish teacher, would sit at his desk directly facing his classroom of students. He had a habit of shifting his eyes downward towards the girls' skirts, as if he was trying to get a glimpse of something forbidden. There was Miss King, the English teacher, who once read my essay to the whole class to show an example of terrible writing. There was Miss Kantar's modern dance course for the girls who wanted an easy way of avoiding gym class, where you were forced to do exercises and play the sports you were no good at. There was Study Hall, which was supervised by Margaret, the wife of one of my cousins. She had a split personality; for it seemed that her personality in the classroom wasn't anything like her personality at the family gatherings where we would occasionally meet. There was Miss Beacon's biology class. One day Miss Beacon was passing bones around for the students to examine when she got one of her rare phone calls. I watched her turn pale when she was told that President Kennedy had been assassinated. There was the Driver's Ed class whose instructor was very confident that I had the ability to parallel park because I had done it once before. "You don't have a problem with parallel parking," he insisted. "If you were able to do it once before, you are able to do it again." They were words that boosted my confidence whenever my confidence needed boosting.

There was Mormon Table in the cafeteria. It became so because the Mormon kids were the early arrivals who came directly from Early Morning Seminary. We sat together and chatted with each other, soaking up the time between Seminary and First Period.

These were the days before girls wore jeans to school. Dresses, skirts and blouses were the norm. There were the skirt-length checks at the gym. The girls were required to kneel on the floor if their skirts appeared to be too short. If the hems didn't touch the floor they were sent home to change. Moms were usually at home to pick up their daughters from school and take them home if the office call was made.

All during high school I missed my father. I often thought of him standing way out in the grape vineyard with his knit cap clutched over his ears, his face leathery from all the sun and sandy wind. He held the pruning shears skillfully ready for the attack. He held them under his arm while he used both hands to wrap the vines around the wires fighting against their strength. Once in a while he lost control. I could see a grapevine hurl its fury at him and smack him in the face on a cold day, making him sob. The colder the day the more it would hurt. As long as he had a reason to sob he would go right on and sob, and never stop. He had no reason to stop.

I hoped Mamma was happier now that I was out of her life. It was a good thing anyway. How long could I keep raiding the Kotex machines in restrooms before I got caught?

I felt guilty that I had it so good. Carl was the only one of the big kids left at the farm. He was a diligent student and worked hard on the farm. On the weekends he sometimes went out with his friends. At the soda shop, where he and his friends hung out, his buddies drank milk shakes but Carl drank ice water because he didn't have money. He missed out on a lot of fun. He was still pleasant to Jensine and everyone else. He never let the family problems defeat him. He was full of goals that he planned to achieve on the highways ahead of him. He decided that the hardships he went through would someday be a thing of the past.

Annabelle and I occasionally boarded the Greyhound Bus and traveled to Fresno to visit the family. As the years wore on the trips got less frequent. Being with the family wasn't the same. Our father wasn't the same. We didn't have to do chores. Washing and drying dishes was no longer a requirement as it had been throughout my childhood. Things were as if we were no longer a part of the Clayland family at the Clayland raisin farm.

The little kids continued to sit around the table, drawing pictures in tablets and reading library books. There was David. In the future he will become the supervisory landscaper of the gardens at one of the Mormon Temples in Utah, and he will become employed as the head landscaper of the grounds at the city courthouse. There was Annette. She will become an elementary schoolteacher and acquire many interests and talents, including art. She will live with her mother for many years after Daddy dies and she will always be there for her needs. There was Diana. One Christmas this little sister tearfully demanded that the fire department be called to help them out in their state of emergency: the family didn't have a Christmas tree. She will become a professional artist and illustrator. There was Spencer. He will become an undercover cop for the city of Denver.

After a few years of working the streets, he will move on to new career heights.

I felt sorry for the little kids. They looked so destitute in their state of poverty. I wondered if their futures were hopeless.

Eight

Derek returned home from his mission to South America and dropped by Uncle Edwin's and Aunt Charlotte's before seeing the Fresno family. He stayed a day or two before going on to higher education. Derek was interested in politics and was planning on some kind of career in it. He and our dad didn't see eye to eye on some things. Derek was obstinate with his political views. He was vocal and he didn't mind stirring up controversy once in a while. His opinions could get boring to listen to. Sometimes his voice had an irritating tone, especially when talking about controversial topics.

He was the kind of person that would leave a trail of possessions behind everywhere he went. He left some of his things in Fresno, some in San Diego at Uncle Edwin's and Aunt Charlotte's, some in San Diego at the grandparents' house, and some in places he had forgotten about.

He was a handsome fellow, but nothing that would drive the girls wild. His eyes were the same hue of blue as his father's. When he smiled his face immediately lost credibility, for his teeth went every which-way. If he wore a business suit his smile made it look contradictory. He could have been one with the grapevines if he ever had the passion for them. When he was a boy, Uncle Edwin paid for orthodontic treatment for him. He had little tolerance for the obnoxious wires on his teeth but he endured them. After the braces came off and the retainer took over, he accidentally dropped it on the ground and stepped on it smashing it to pieces. Uncle Edwin didn't know about his losing the retainer and it never got replaced. His teeth eventually reverted back to their natural state.

Derek clung to his religion and valued his faith emphatically. His religion was his armor, he was determined to not falter. He liked to read faith-promoting stories. He was always interested in things that were not of mortality. He became the author of an article about the pre-existence that got published in the Church's official monthly magazine for adult members.

There was a kind of sadness about Derek, almost an air of defeat about him that begged to become his nature. But he could still laugh and play. He teased little kids, let them take rides on his back. He got good at making Donald Duck sounds. He had a hearty laugh. Derek had a sense of humor and was a willing volunteer for participation in any prank.

Tom was back from his mission at the time I turned twelve years old. Unknown to me he had in his possession an enormous blown Ostrich egg that he brought back from South America. It was to be the prop in a prank. It was my chore to gather the chicken eggs out of the chicken coup, no arduous task because it was only enough to feed the family and give away the excess to friends and family. Derek and Tom placed the shocking egg on a chicken's nest one morning before I went to gather the eggs. The two brothers positioned themselves near the coup and acted like they were clearing weeds from the vegetable garden. They didn't want to miss the opportunity of seeing the expression on my face when I came running out of the coup in a frenzy of excitement and wild wonder. They were able to view just what they were after. After they had their big laugh, I wondered what the chickens thought of the mutant egg.

Derek dressed up in a Santa Claus suit to pose for a group picture for his school yearbook. He had a lot to look forward to in life and sometimes enjoyed tinting it with humor. He got irate and emotional when he thought about the trials of the family. There were some young ladies interested in him, but he felt insecure about having any kind of a long-term relationship that might lead to marriage. Derek understood the expansiveness of eternity and the commitments that went with it.

He enjoyed becoming educated. He was interested in learning a variety of subjects. He liked astronomy, history, physics, anthropology and zoology. He was the kind of a person that couldn't resist a shelf of books. If a book didn't look very interesting to him, he picked it up and scanned it anyway. He liked to share the things he learned with his friends and family. The National Geographic was his favorite magazine. He enjoyed watching documentaries on television.

Derek's grades were okay. He took a campus job to help defray costs of obtaining a degree in Political Science, a degree he would eventually come to regret because it turned out to be useless for obtaining employment. He still attended school when Carl and I arrived to begin our education. Occasionally while walking between classes the siblings crossed each other's paths and exchanged glances that no one else could ever comprehend.

Nine

In 1972 the posterity of Henry Clayland were spread over the country. Several of them were married and raising their families. A few of the sons and daughters were still in school. Henry and Jensine still lived at the raisin farm, struggling to survive.

The barn looked the same: still unpainted and still missing the boards. Henry retired the raisin sifter to the barn when he learned that the sand that was unintentionally swept onto the trays when they got rolled was expected to be present in the shipment crates. The buyers took it into consideration when they set the prices.

The toilet was still incapable of standard flushing methods because of the plumbing situation. The boys' room became sleeping quarters for visiting sons and daughters. There wasn't a more suitable place to put them and the grandchildren. The modern kitchen range wasn't looking so modern anymore. The color on the panel wasn't the trend for the current year.

Jensine appeared to be a little more relaxed. She erased all thoughts of ever having a house built in the middle of the almond orchard. The open septic tank below the kitchen window was covered with boards. A pine tree that Henry had planted in a previous year blocked the view of one end of it. He planted the sapling after the Christmas when young Diana declared the state of emergency. Their intention was to cut it down the following Christmas but they decided not to. By the time the next Christmas came, Diana was a little more mature and could handle not having a Christmas tree inside the house. Now the tree was large and it blended in well with the landscape.

Smokey, the old family dog, was seeing the last of his days. He was one of the puppies born in the barn to Lucky, our first farm dog. There was never a more wonderful farm dog.

Motorists in cars passing through the intersection by the south vineyard could see rampant branches being choked by the Bermuda grass that won the battle long ago. If Henry was a young man, he would have plowed out the whole mess, grapevines and all. He would have converted the land to almonds.

The goldfish tank/cow trough was gone. Hamburger, the cow, got sold. They never would have eaten her. The fruit trees on the plot between Grapevine and the house were bigger than ever. They didn't get pruned every year, so the yield was poor.

The property began its ninth year of being on the market. The little kids that were left at home considered submitting the data to the Guinness Book of World Records. No one was very interested in buying the run-down place and its neglected vineyards. A few years back they had almost had a sale, but everyone that bought property in that part of the county preferred to buy northeast of the city. The growth was going in that direction, as were property values.

Uncle Edwin retired from the medical profession and went into the oil business. He and Aunt Charlotte left their breath-taking house in San Diego and moved to Maryland. Their only son was a conscripted soldier in Vietnam. They were terrified of losing him.

Uncle Samuel and his wife, Aunt Mari, had only two kids of Aunt Hannah's left to finish rearing. Aunt Hannah was the aunt who got killed by the drunken truck driver.

Except for David, the little kids were still at the farm. Except for Derek, all the big kids were married and had children. Derek was in Vietnam temporarily working for the Red Cross. I had found someone who looked beyond my silent inner turmoil and married him. I decided to put my emotional afflictions behind me and try to feel normal, though it was difficult.

Ten

The people that eventually bought the raisin farm never paid them all they were supposed to, a broken promise that was too complicated and expensive to take any action against. The buyers justified their non-payment by explaining that they were not able to make any money from the crop. Henry and Jensine understood their predicament so they ended up taking out a bank loan in order to come up with their required share of closing expenses for the house they purchased in American Fork, Utah.

They got a good deal on the house they bought. It was a small cinder-block house set within the sloping reaches of Mount Timpanogos. It had a carport, a basement, and a small bathroom. Aside from the financial strain of settlement, life was pleasant in American Fork. Jensine had a full-time job that she liked, and she loved the people she worked with. She was thankful to be off the farm and she was thankful that Henry finally supported her in her desire to return to Utah.

Old friends informed Henry and Jensine that a mobile home was stationed in the foreground of the condemned farmhouse at Fresno. The boys' room was a pile of rubble, and I think the rickety farmhouse became the new tool shed.

Henry retired. Social security income and Jensine's paycheck sustained them.

Henry puttered around the yard a lot. He maintained the gardens that he and Jensine had installed immediately upon their arrival at American Fork. Each day he sat on his "thinking rock," a massive boulder that overlooked the road in front of the house. He liked to sit on the rock and watch the traffic go by. Sometimes he called it his grumbling rock, a place where he could go and grumble.

Henry began to feel the effects of the steady diet of grease burgers. The years of artery abuse began to set in. Cold weather bothered him, the altitude bothered him, his asthma bothered him, and his rheumatism was getting the best of him. He didn't get around too well and he didn't think he could make it through another winter. The doctor informed him that he had an enlarged heart. The condition of his heart was the reason he was continually out of breath, and it was why he wasn't able to walk down the road to the nearby church. Henry wasn't too concerned about it. Life begins and then life ends. You're born, you live, and then you die. No one can escape death. Why would he even want to?

The family convened in August of that year for a family reunion. It was the first time the family had been together since they lived at the raisin farm. There were so many grandchildren that Henry lost count, lots of sons-in-law and daughters-in-law, some that need replacing.

Family pictures were being taken. "Everyone stand together and smile for a moment while pictures are being made." The little kids stood next to the big kids. It was the first time they stood together. It was a start.

Henry's collection of family records were stored in the basement of the small cinder-block house. His lifetime supply of photographs and negatives remained stored within the filing cabinet below the desktop, protected from the brightness of the sunlight and the mustiness of the atmosphere. He hoped that everything would remain the same after his death, at least until the time some of his posterity became interested in it. Hopefully someone would take the initiative to make copies of some of it.

It was time for everyone to go separate ways. It was time to bid farewell to his sons and daughters.

I put my kids in the car for the long trip home. After I gave my father a long and lingering hug, I got in the car and unrolled the window. The fragrance of the climbing rose bushes that hugged the walls of the house lent itself to my father's approach. I knew he wanted to say one more goodbye. He didn't look well. My emotions stirred, and I became torn between reality and denial. I looked into his eyes to find reassurance, but there wasn't any. His eyes seemed to elude the assault of age and disease; they retained the same brilliance I had always remembered.

Should I say what a devoted daughter would say to her father upon his deathbed, but with roses in the background? Or should I speak words of encouragement that would make him feel comfortable?

He spoke first. "I'm glad you came to live with me."

It was no time for intense dialogue nor was there any need for it. I smiled. "I love you too, Daddy."

The familiar words, "I'm glad you came to live with me," grasped me in the setting of emotional uncertainty. It was always his way of letting me know that he loved me.

He spoke the words each time we departed company, and he wrote the words to me in his letters. What else could be said? Henry backed away from the idling car. Then we drove away.

The funeral was six weeks later. All of Henry's sons and daughters were there. As the nine siblings were conversing with each other a startling discovery was made. We learned that our father had spoken his tacit expression of affection, "I'm glad you came to live with me" to each of his nine children.

Thirty-one years after she made her solemn commitments to her husband, Jensine stood in silence at his grave-site. She composed the words in her mind that portrayed the relationship she had with him. The casket, waiting for the mourners to leave so it could descend into the earth, stood lifeless like a statue, but full of meaning. She cast her eyes downward in defense of her sorrow. This was a man who had betrayed her heart. In the torment of her years of unselfish commitments, she spoke with a voice full of sorrow. "If he doesn't want me in the next life, maybe someone else will."

Eleven

The American Fork family settled into a routine after the funeral. The sons and daughters of Henry decided to memorialize the words that displayed the unconditional and reassuring love of our father. They were etched on his headstone under his name, birth, and death date: WE'RE GLAD WE CAME TO LIVE WITH YOU.

Almost everyone in the family accepted the decision to bury him in American Fork. We considered moving his body to the cemetery in Orange County in California where he had a purchased plot next to Grace's. But no one would ever have been there to tend his grave, just as no one was there to tend Grace's grave.

Henry's easy chair was removed from the living room. There was no evidence of Henry on the main level. But down in the cluttered office room of the basement the spirit of Henry was everywhere. His makeshift desk had been relocated to a secluded spot in the corner. The top of his desk was almost as it was when he left it: a tin can full of pencils and dried-up pens, and miscellaneous items scattered on the desktop. Henry's life radiated from inside the drawers of the desk where the family records, journals, letters, and photographs were kept.

I didn't get out there as often as I used to. I was busy with my own family. Raising children was a taxing task, not to be taken lightly. My children were my focus, they were my joy and my sorrow. I had in my possession my own collection of family history. The brown-tinted photograph of my mother was stored in a trunk, put away so I could avoid the anguish of my past. I had the stories that my relatives wrote about my mother. I had the letters my mother wrote from the hospital. They were folded up long ago and stored so that I could continue to walk the path that I had chosen. And I knew that I would never throw any of it away.

Twelve

Derek took Suzanne, his betrothed, to the Sierras to meet the family. The flickering fire of the campfire cast a lovely glow upon her face as Derek's siblings bestowed their judgments upon her. Some of the siblings judged her as kind, tender and as warm as the fire that threw its heat upon her. Was her kindness as generous as the warmth of the fire? The family hoped so. Derek was approaching his mid-thirties. What really was Derek's attraction to Suzanne? Where was the passion? Why didn't they look at each other? Body language is everything. These were thoughts that ran through heads. Love is supposed to come softly and without sting, without malice and contempt. The family members reminded themselves that who Derek chose to marry was not anyone's business.

After their wedding in a Mormon temple, Derek and Suzanne settled in a small farming town in Colorado. He got a job with a company doing data entry and she worked for County Social Services. The two of them took in several foster children during the time they remained together. Suzanne was a loving person. She had a glowing kind of countenance for all the little disadvantaged children under her protection. But something went wrong along the path to their eternal goals. It was probably the lack of passion we had noticed in both of them. It could have been anguish and malice creeping in from Suzanne's past, as well as from Derek's. Perhaps Suzanne merely wanted a child out of the relationship, one she could always keep and not have to give back to someone. In any case, tensions between the two accelerated. In a state of pregnancy, Suzanne drove Derek out of the house, out of her life, and out of the life of their child yet to be born.

Wendy was born only slightly too soon. Suzanne selected the name without Derek's opinion. She sent him a birth announcement and a picture of the baby with pierced ears. Derek was hurt when he learned of his daughter's birth in such an insensitive way. He was furious that Suzanne pierced the baby's ears.

Divorces were much too common an occurrence in almost every family. Though temple marriage for eternity was supposed to be the norm in Mormon families, many of them experienced the agony of separation and divorce. The Lord understood his sons and daughters well enough to know that sometimes reprise was necessary for endurance. On the other hand, He wanted marriages to endure through trials that may come to them for the sake of the children born to husband and wife. Mortal death was not the end for the opportunities in expressions of forgiveness and understanding. The family members supported Derek and stood by him in his trials.

After the divorce, Derek moved to a metropolitan area for more secure work as there wasn't much work opportunity where he lived. As it usually goes, he maintained some contact with his daughter in spite of having to deal with the agony of communication with Wendy's mother. Derek's fatherhood wasn't getting off to a good start. He sent Suzanne some child support payments. Suzanne had full custody of Wendy. Derek had visitation rights. The dictates of the social system determined that occasional visitation was sufficient for Derek, and that he deserved no more than that. One weekend, Derek drove three hundred miles to be with his daughter, a visitation that had been agreed upon with Suzanne. When he got there, Suzanne had taken Wendy out of town. Derek didn't have the opportunity to be with his daughter that weekend.

Divorce proceedings became finalized. Suzanne was free at last. She was a confident woman who didn't need a man in her life. She had friends that were girls. She had a good income so was able to support her child and her foster children with or without child support from her ex-husband and father to her child. ***Time heals all wounds.***

Derek met Marlene during a picnic at a Church social. She was a secretary in a finance office and a divorced mother of two sons. She and Derek began to date. Before long Derek once again felt the stirrings of commitment, caring, passion, and responsibility. Her two little boys were included in the future he was looking forward to with Marlene.

Derek and Marlene dated for a few years. Marlene often broke up with Derek. She didn't know the reason and she couldn't explain it. The courtship was always the off-and-on kind. In spite of her inconsistency, Derek maintained his devotion towards her. He finally proposed marriage at a time when Marlene was feeling stable. They became betrothed. Derek's heart was filled with elation, and he looked forward to living in a state of bliss with Marlene. He rejoiced at the opportunity of being a step-father to her two sons. But the courtship wavered as they continued their relationship. One day, Marlene broke off the engagement. Because Derek still loved her and thought her remarkable, they maintained the romance. Derek was convinced that Marlene was his one and only soul-mate, eternally and forever, never to be disregarded.

But there was something about Marlene that disturbed him. He analyzed the situation and decided he must mandate a solution to the unsteady relationship. He presented his proposal to Marlene.

"Marlene, there is a choice you must make. Either we stop seeing each other, or marry me now. I can no longer live like this. I can no longer live with the inconsistency of your devotion."

Marlene thought about it for a while. It would be nice if the two boys had a father again. They lost contact with their birth father. The boys thought Derek was great and they had already bonded with him. Derek held his breath the whole time Marlene was thinking about it. He really hoped she would say yes. Derek should have let his breath out before she gave her answer, and he should have taken off running as fast as he could.

Marlene accepted Derek's proposal of eternal marriage. They were wed in the nearby Mormon Temple. The ideal little family, you would think. But the problem was that Marlene continued with the off-and-on trend of attention and affection for Derek. Sometimes she was on, and sometimes she was off with her ego, id, and superego. "Off" appeared more often than "on" until there was no "on" left at all. Just because they got married, it didn't mean she would change. Somewhere during an "on" moment Marlene got pregnant. At one stretch of the "off" moments Derek ventured on a business deal that someone he knew promised would be a boon to his livelihood.

Against the objections of Marlene, Derek quit his current job and left his new family to proceed with his share of the business responsibilities. Several weeks later, he came back with nothing in his pockets. He admitted defeat, but was able to find occasional employment.

After the incident Marlene began to feel waves in her marriage. She braced for the inevitable. She convinced Derek that they should move to a more metropolitan area. They made the difficult move. They found an apartment near her family. It wasn't as easy for him to find work as it was for her. She immediately picked up a new job. He found one that wasn't very good.

Their baby, Cole, was born. He became very sickly after contacting an infection while in the hospital. He had to stay in Intensive Care Unit until he was past danger. Everyone was worried that he would be brain damaged if he lived. But the day finally came when baby Cole was well enough to be released from the hospital. The family would never be the same.

Severe financial trials continued for Derek and Marlene. The medical bills and all kinds of other bills came at a steady pace. There never was a time in Derek's life when he had earned very much. He always made enough to get by and to meet his obligations. There was a time when money wasn't the most important thing in the world to him. In order for him to maintain his integrity, money suddenly became very important to him.

It was time for Marlene to end the marriage. She had a secure job and her family lived nearby. She and Derek separated. Derek's bonding experience with his newborn was once again denied him. Divorce was pending and fatherhood was fading. ***Time heals all wounds, and eternity lasts forever.***

Was that where we were to meet our little Cole and Wendy, somewhere in the expanse of eternity? They were both assigned to us, our little group called family. On earth they were always lost to us. Two little hearts turned from the heart of their father, heritage diminished. *They know not who sheds tears for them.* One moment of silence at Serenity's feet.

Derek felt like a fool. How did he ever think that she would change? After all the times she had broken up with him, why did he think it would be any different after they were married? Marlene found a good divorce attorney and demanded a hefty settlement.

Derek felt like he was going to collapse. He didn't know how he would be able to meet all of his obligations. He was going to be making two support payments now, both at different households. He was able to deal with Wendy's some of the time, but what about Cole's? He didn't have a good enough job to cover it. He didn't know what he was going to do.

Thirteen

Derek heard about a good psychologist. He decided he would pay a visit. He needed to know what was wrong with him. Why wasn't he able to stay married? Why was he feeling so unstable? Why did he continue to be so foolish?

He waited nervously in the waiting room. He had never before been to a psychologist. He guessed he should have gone a long time ago. He had no self-esteem. He felt very abnormal. He cried often when no one could see him. Songs kept coming to his mind. Lately he couldn't get them out of his mind.

He almost turned around to walk out of the room. Why was he here? This was a stupid idea.

"Mr. Clayland."

Derek stood up. He was about to run out the door, but he had already made the appointment. He didn't have any right to spend money on himself, but he decided to proceed.

In the doctor's office, Derek sat on a brocade sofa of subtle colors. The room had a comfortable decor. The lights were dim and the atmosphere relaxing. He already felt better. He hadn't realized that the psychologist would be a woman.

"Why don't we start by telling me a little about you?"

"My second marriage just failed. I have two children. One is just an infant and the other one is five years old."

"So why are you here?" The psychologist was taking notes.

"Because things in my life aren't going so well. My whole life is becoming messed up."

"Tell me about your two failed marriages. What was it that attracted you to these two women in the first place? Let's start with the first one. Give me a little of her background."

Derek stared at his hands. "Well, she was married once before. It was a very short marriage, no children. But she took several foster children into her home. After we were married we continued to take them in. I think she felt the need to rescue."

"That's interesting. Do you know anything about her childhood?"

"Yes, she claims that she had been treated badly through her young life, mostly by men."

The psychologist nodded as she took more notes. "Now tell me about your second marriage. What kind of a childhood did your second wife have?"

"The same kind. She says she had been treated badly by men."

"So it appears that you're attracted to women that have been battered around by men? Do you see a pattern here?"

Derek took a few seconds to absorb the question she just asked him. "I guess I never really thought about it. I mean, I never considered it to be the criteria for a relationship. I never went up to a woman and asked her if she'd ever been abused and battered by men and then decide to have a relationship with her."

She smiled. "Yes, I understand what you're saying. But as you got more acquainted with each of them, and they became more open to discuss it, you learned, you empathized…"

Derek interrupted, "So is that why I'm so screwed up? Is that why I can't be a real father to my two children, because I chose to marry women who had been treated badly by men?"

Derek took a few minutes to explain to the psychologist the history of the marriages. The doctor of psychology made certain that the tape recorder was functioning properly.

After taking some more notes she looked up. "Let's try to figure out why you're attracted to women who have these kind of issues. From what you've explained, it seems that they both have had problems with bonding with men because of the way they have been treated."

The discussion was making Derek feel rather perplexed, and he was becoming curious as to what the counsel would be for him.

Changing the subject, the doctor continued. "Let's talk about your childhood."

Derek moaned. "No, I don't think I could. I had a severely abnormal childhood, far away from ordinary. It would be too hard and too complex to dig into it."

"If you want to know what your problem with women is, then you might need to address it. Tell me about your mother, and then I want to hear about your father."

Derek dropped his head as if all the weight of his pain was in his skull. Then he reminded himself that he wasn't a little boy. Though he gained some self-control, he didn't think he would be able to talk about his mother.

The psychologist saw his discomfort. "Why don't you step back into the waiting room for a while? There isn't anyone in there. Come back when you're ready, then we'll talk about your mother."

Derek went back to the waiting room. He considered running out of the office, down the road, never to come back. He didn't think he could talk about his mother. He could never get through it.

He decided he had to at some time. Feeling calmer, he went back into the comfortable room, where the therapist was making an effort to tame the hurricane that was raging inside him.

"I loved my mother more than I could ever explain to anyone. She always made me feel very special. I used to think that I was her favorite child. One time, I told my older brother that I always thought I was her favorite child. He told me he always thought that he was her favorite. She used to sing songs to me. Lately the songs keep coming to me, and I sing them over and over in my head."

"So you always thought that you were her favorite, all through your childhood?"

Derek shook his head, "Not exactly."

"Are you saying that you did have some conflict with your mother?"

He looked up. "When I was six years old I had a problem with her. She died."

"You were only six years old!"

"Yeah," he replied.

"Was it just you and your brother that she left?"

"No, also my little sister, Annabelle, and my little brother Carl, and my baby sister Camilla."

The therapist paused. She raised her eyebrows in a gesture of concern. "That's five! Your mother died and left five little children?"

"Yeah," he responded with anguish in his voice.

"How did she die?"

"She just had my baby sister. She had problems with having the baby. She didn't die right away, but she was never well after the baby came. She actually died in a hospital. No one in my family would talk about it. It was always too painful for anyone to discuss her death. I don't even know exactly what happened. My Dad told me that she choked on something."

She kept writing. "How old were the other children?"

"Carl was about seventeen months, Annabelle was four years old. Tom was eleven."

"Do you remember when you last saw your mother?"

"She was in her bed. My father got ready to take her to the hospital. He was going to take her out of town. A babysitter came over. Dad picked my mother up to carry her out the door. Then she told me to do something that I've always tried to do for her."

"What did she say to you?"

"She told me to take care of my brothers and sisters."

The doctor told Derek he would need to come back to talk about it some more. Derek made an appointment for the next day.

When he went back to the psychologist, he felt a little more relaxed.

The doctor of psychology told Derek they would talk more about his mother later. She wanted to talk about his father for a while. "Do you think your parents were happy with their marriage?"

"My parents loved each other. I had a happy home. We lived in a little apartment in a hotel complex that they owned and managed."

"How did your father react to her death?"

"When she died he was never the same. My relatives who knew him before my mother died would swear it. I swear it too because I can remember."

The psychologist nodded. "I can understand how her death must have grieved him. He loved her and now he had their five little children to be solely responsible for. That fact would leave any man devastated. Losing her and at the same time gaining the burden of raising their little children would make almost any responsible man become distraught to the point of psychological dysfunction."

"Are you saying that my father had severe psychological disorders for the rest of his life?"

"I think you can answer that question yourself." The therapist wanted Derek to reach his own conclusions.

Derek paused for a moment to calm down. "After we went back to the apartment there was so much sadness. Then one day we left it. My father told me that the child welfare agency, or some kind of agency like that, was trying to take us away from him, and that was why he had to leave us. He told me that he would come back for me. I went to live with one of my aunts and her family for a few months."

Derek began to gain some self-control. "A few months later, my father came back for me just as he had promised. I was glad to see him but he gave me something I didn't want. He gave me a new mother. I didn't want a new mother. Having no mother was better than having a different mother. I was so angry at him. He didn't even ask me if I wanted a different mother."

"How old were you then?"

"Seven."

"Did you get along with her?"

He shook his head as he wiped a tear off his cheek. "No, why would I want to get along with anyone who was trying to take my mother's place? I never wanted her to be my mother. I didn't want her to be my brothers' and sisters' mother. No one could ever replace our real mother."

"Did you try to do anything that would turn the others away from your stepmother?"

"When I think back on it I was trying to help them all. I was supposed to help them. It was confusing. There were conflicts. I can't remember too well. I remember failing, always failing. I was overwhelmed by my responsibilities."

The doctor paused to make sure Derek was finished. "What did your father do about it?"

"Sort of ignored it, like there wasn't anything he could do about it. He escaped into genealogical research. I don't remember him ever doing genealogy until we lived in Burbank."

"Let's get back to your mother. Do you realize what your mother was asking of you when she last spoke to you? The problem you had with your stepmother was that you were trying to fulfill your mother's last request. That's where the dilemma lies. The last time you saw your mother she asked you to do something that was way out of your territory. It was wrong of her to ask you to take care of your brothers and sisters. That was asking too much of a little six year old child."

Derek looked confused. He slumped onto the armrest of the sofa. This was something he was going to have to think about for a few minutes. "So am I supposed to be angry?"

"Yes, you're supposed to be very angry. I give you permission. But she was your mother who died, and you don't want to be angry with an angel. Am I right?"

Derek nodded. "I could never be angry with my mother, no matter what she said."

"But you'll have to be if you want to get better. Get angry with her. It's okay."

"Am I supposed to just say it, and then all my problems will disappear?"

The therapist pointed across the room. "Do you see that chair over there? Throw it at the wall. It will show her that you're angry with her. Show her that's the way you feel about her."

Derek went over to pick up the chair. He threw it violently against the wall. He had never been angry with his mother before. It felt strange to be showing his animosity to his mother. He wondered if she might be watching him. He decided that she probably wasn't, but it felt good to show anger anyway.

The therapist continued. "As far as the problem you have with women is concerned, you feel as though you've failed your siblings because you weren't able to fulfill your mother's last request. You've projected your feelings of guilt upon your choices of women. You became attracted to women who had emotional problems because of abuse. Don't get me wrong, I'm not saying that all women fail to overcome abuse. You happened to choose two women who weren't able to bond to men because they didn't recover from the bad experiences they had in their past."

This was all quite a bit for Derek to absorb. The therapist allowed a lengthy pause so that Derek could ponder what she said.

After a few minutes she went on. "You wanted to make up for your failures. You were trying to relieve your guilt to your God and to your mother by helping someone else overcome her painful past. You tried to be a husband, stepfather, and foster father with women who couldn't accept your help. And you wanted to replace the guilt of failure by taking care of children who were deprived of fathers."

Now Derek understood himself better.

Fourteen

Adriana was a member of the single's congregation at the Church that Derek began attending after he separated from Marlene. Adriana noticed him, but he didn't notice her. All he could think about was his crumbling marriage and his mounting responsibilities. He was trying to overcome his heartache.

Adriana had seen him previously at a few Church activities and socials before he left to get married. She remembered secretly wishing that she had claimed him first. She didn't think Derek wanted to talk to her, ever. Now his countenance seemed to be tainted with despair. Why hadn't she gone up to him before he disappeared; why hadn't she been forthright with him: "You're supposed to be mine, not hers." She put the thoughts of regret aside. Obviously the marriage didn't stick.

Adriana was thirty-five years old and, unlike many of her single friends, had never been married. She was born and raised in a small rural Utah town nestled at the edge of a national forest. A grocery store and a gas station were the only two enterprises in the town. The community was eighty-five percent Mormon. Her widowed mother lived on a farm that had been in her family since the pioneer days. Adriana had a comfortable job working as a secretary in the big cities. She didn't make a lot of money, but she had enough for a car, her living expenses and a little savings. She was satisfied with her income.

Derek worked temporary jobs and did construction work in Utah. He searched for steady work in the computer industry but the jobs didn't always pan out. During his separation from Marlene, he and Adriana sometimes chatted in the halls at the Church. He decided to ask her out when the divorce was finalized.

After the divorce, he and Adriana dated. Adriana never claimed to be a victim of any unkindness towards her, and she didn't have any children. They fell in love and got married in the church building located down the road from where Adriana lived. Adriana's family was delighted, as was Derek's.

Hints of promising job opportunities in the Houston area encouraged the newlywed couple to uproot and relocate. They sold Adriana's furniture to offset the expenses of moving. Derek didn't have anything of any value to move. They left for Houston. It was the first time Adriana lived away from Utah.

They both found work in Houston. Derek worked for a construction company and Adriana worked as a secretary. They looked forward to an eternal state of happiness. They were frugal in their lifestyle. They were both tight with the money. They met some financial obligations. Adriana clipped coupons. They lived in an apartment in the suburbs on the south side of the city.

After spending a year in Houston, Derek got laid off his job. Houston had been experiencing a downward spiral in employment opportunities. Then they moved to Northern Virginia for work because jobs were in better supply in the D.C. metropolis. They moved in with relatives for a while until things got stable. Their love and devotion for each other got them through their trials. Affordable housing was difficult to find. Adriana got pregnant.

Andrew was born. Adriana was delighted to be a mother. Derek was thrilled to have another opportunity to be a father and be able to finally take part in the life of one of his children. Adriana had a steady job. Leaving the baby with a sitter was against her beliefs, but she had no choice. They were in the same boat that a lot of people were in. Derek worked both construction and temporary office jobs. They were making it, but times were tough. Obligations that screamed at them were slipping away, becoming out of control.

Derek was able to find a teaching job at a high school. He taught American History and Spanish. He didn't have a teaching degree at the time. The school district offered to provide tuition assistance to help him get one.

Then Mariah was born. Since childcare would cost more than what she was able to earn, Adriana quit her job. Derek was supposed to be supporting a family scattered all over the place on a teaching job that didn't bring in enough money. He continued to be faithful and pray to the Lord. He tried to maintain some optimism over his trials. He convinced himself that the opposition he faced was for a reason, and that time would correct it.

Eugene B. Seaman
1934

Grace's Funeral Day

Serenity 1996

Serenity 1999

Serenity
2001

Serenity 2002

Serenity 2013

Serenity 2015

Fifteen

Serenity had been artfully and skillfully sculptured. Her artist examined his creation and was pleased. To him her message was achieved: the Statue of Friendship for the United States Government, to remain as long as friendship may endure. Jose' Clara created her in honor of a lifelong friend. Serenity never made the honor roll for noteworthy national monuments. As far as her name went, she was as typical as the unknown creator who bore her.

In spite of her insignificance in the catalogues of national monuments, her gracefulness invited tranquility for all who stood before her. She was there when young lovers spoke words of affection and commitment. At her feet they made plans for their futures. It was as it should be, for that was her mission.

She was there for the mothers and the fathers of the nation as they guided their children along the paths that they must go. Along her path, the children broke away in haste the moment they came into her view. They ran to her and climbed upon her lap. She allowed their happiness to soar: they will not always be children. She remained steadfast, unmovable, and dependable, unlike her world around her.

Serenity was there when the dignitaries of the world strolled the path before her. The dignitaries spoke words of brotherhood and goodwill. The world was at their mercy.

Under the light of the moon, the cast of the stars, the brilliance of what the sun offered, Serenity experienced the decades in the stationary spot that her government assigned her. She tried to remain true to her mission of friendship. Histories unfolded before her while she remained stalwart in her fortitude.

Within the walls of her surroundings, upon the carpet of her world, she witnessed the corruption of new generations. She was there when the promises were broken. She was there through the wars and the rumors of wars. She was there through the demise of everything that was once beautiful and good. She saw the beauty of her surroundings decay, the beauty of the world that was meant to be. Throughout the years and the turning of the seasons, Serenity became despondent. Her uninviting embrace, her trampled face, her torn arm, and her tattered gown became the ensign of everything wrong that once was right. The little children no longer climbed upon her lap. They turned their faces away in fear: *A lady is supposed to have a clean face, and a washed gown without scribbles all over it. She is supposed to have a nose, and two hands, not one.*

Within the decades of her existence, she listened to the weeping of the children who had their hearts turned from the hearts of their fathers. She listened to the weeping of the fathers who had their hearts turned from the hearts of their children.

She gazed upon the ugliness of crime and all its painful messages. She saw men and women destroy their potentials. She saw and heard the weeping of the defiled. She saw death arrive in a blanket of hatred.

Serenity's thoughtful gaze remained fixed upon Sixteenth Street. The neglect and destruction of her property betrayed her purpose. Traffic noises and other sounds of metropolis increased since the time she was created. The flow of the fountain made way for the grime of the city. At times, drug dealers used the shade of the trees to make their illegal exchanges to provide for illegal drug abusers. The honesty and integrity of Serenity's face was stolen by vandals and tarnished by pollution.

The people at the park walk her path and pause before her. Looks of surprise sweep over them. They think to themselves: "This is a work of art that is worthy to be dubbed a national monument!" They reverently revise their perception: She is no longer worthy, but they understand that she once was.

The people wonder about her face. Surely her skin hasn't always been pocked. How many different noses have been pasted upon her face? What is the true nature of her sunken eye sockets? What should be the style of her hair? Her gown hasn't always been streaked with grime and insulted with graffiti!

Serenity's true artistic features continued to remain a mystery to those who strolled before her.

Sixteen

Derek thought he could get work in the metropolitanism of the Utah valley. It was a high growth industrial area. The computer industry was booming. He was sure he could pick up a good job. He had been employed as a computer programmer a time or two. They planned on settling down somewhere, something to rent until they could buy a home under a first time buyer program. Being closer to his other offspring was a worthy consideration. He was full of wishful visits. Being in Virginia wasn't the answer as far as his other children were concerned. He needed to be in closer proximity to both of them, so that he could begin a plan for connecting with them.

They packed their possessions and optimistically began their trip back west. Hope was in the horizons they faced. When they arrived in Utah, Derek dropped Adriana and the children off at her mother's home, located near the canyon lands. Then he proceeded to search for work. He was a little nervous about it. He was floating around in his forties, had been for years. His job résumé looked a little shaky. He didn't think it was very serious.

After six years of searching for work, Derek began to get discouraged about finding suitable employment. His family still lived at the farm waiting for him to come get them so they could live together as a family. The best he could do was to visit them on weekends. He looked forward to every minute he could spend with them. He wished he could do it in his own home.

The friends he had made while wandering around in the big cities began to criticize him for neglecting his family's needs. It came in the form of a sneer, a turn of the head, and a cold response to conversation. Ostracism diluted his self-esteem and petrified his soul.

He worked at a dog food factory until more suitable work could be found. He was sure that one day he would find a good job so he could bring his family together again. He took it upon himself to learn the Italian language on the factory production lines so the work wouldn't be tedious and boring. He also worked for temporary employment agencies. He worked any job he was able to find. He was far behind in the child support payments. He clung to the hope that one day he would catch up. Occasionally he sought employment out of the state. His luck there wasn't any better. If necessary, he was willing to take jobs out of the area, but he preferred to stay as close to his responsibilities as he could.

He lived under a thin shell attached to the back of his pickup truck. A small butane heater kept away the chill of the winter nights. Adriana cried a lot. She cried every time he called her mother's home to talk to her and the kids. He felt the thousands of tears that she shed.

Even though he wasn't financially supportive of them, he made efforts to restore communication with the children of the other marriages. He and Adriana gave up on attempting partial custody of his children. The efforts were fruitless.

At our nation's capital, Serenity, the Statue of Friendship, continued to remain disturbed, abused, and polluted.

One year, Derek and Adriana bought Christmas presents for Cole. They put the gifts in a shipping box and sent them to him. Marlene returned the unopened package. Derek and Adriana wept together. When they said their prayers that night they prayed to be comforted.

Derek and Adriana had an opportunity to move to a large city. They planned on using their tax refund as a down payment on an apartment. Adriana would have been able to get a job in town and help out with the finances. Then one of their creditors put a claim on the money. They had to stay with the mother-in-law for a few more years.

Derek began to feel embarrassed about his résumé. He decided to try his luck in Los Angeles. The goals of becoming a father to his other children again faded into obscurity.

He felt like the loser of the century. He was reminded of it each morning when he sat up from his mattress, wedged between the inside walls of his pickup camper. He was reminded of it every time he fought the chilly nights by lighting the small butane furnace that was jammed between the cab and the seat. He was reminded of it when he filled the gasoline tank, thinking that it was destined to be its last fill.

When the pickup broke down he managed to coast it to the nearby parking lot of a Mormon Church: The Church of Jesus Christ of Latter-day Saints. It was one of the many Churches that enhanced the residential neighborhoods of Anaheim. He parked it in the far corner of the back parking lot, out of the way, less of a rebel among all the vehicles that would typically be admired.

Being a Wednesday, Derek knew that an activity or a meeting would be going on inside the Church building. He was well acquainted with the Mormon religion. He was nurtured in the faith. His mission for the Church in South America had been an unforgettable experience. He faithfully had served in every Church calling when he wasn't a wanderer wondering why society was beating him so unmercifully.

He was familiar with typical Mormon schedules. The youth groups met for Boy Scouts and Young Women's meetings. In the recreation hall, a game of basketball invited the young men to indulge in the spirit of competition. In the classrooms, ladies met for Relief Society: the women's auxiliary meeting that consisted of mini lessons, workshops that taught parenthood skills, household hints, crafts, or reminders of the duties and obligations that befell women.

Derek waited for evening to come. In the meantime, he walked to a gas station to wash his face and hands in the sink of the men's room. He always made an effort to look clean and well-groomed in spite of his wrinkled clothing. He carried his small sack of grooming supplies, tucked inside the front of his coat. He didn't want motorists passing by to assume that he was carrying anything questionable. He didn't want them to come to the conclusion that he was a drunken sloth who was bent on self-destruction. He always knew better than to consume anything alcoholic. Alcoholic beverages and illegal drugs were offensive to God. He was always determined to honor the Word of Wisdom, the doctrine of healthful living that was found in the Doctrine and Covenants, the Church's book of basic doctrine.

After he finished at the service station, he strolled to a supermarket to see if anyone might be handing out samples of food. It didn't seem to be the right day for it. He reached into his pocket for the small amount of money that he had. He bought a box of Wheat Chex with his change. He had found that eating a handful of the Chex and drinking plenty of water afterwards was enough to satisfy and sustain him for a few hours.

As he advanced towards the Church doors, he felt confident he would have permission to retire for a few nights in the parking lot. Brother Derek Clayland entered the Church so he could ask the bishop for permission to park his broken-down pickup in the parking lot. He stopped in the lobby to listen to the usual sounds coming from the recreation room. The noises of competition emanated from the basketball courts. It made him remember his own days of being young and full of competitive energy.

He suddenly longed to have his youth back so that he could have a chance to start over again. Standing in the Church's lounge, while waiting for his next decisive move, his thoughts began to ponder the ways in which he could have made his life different than it was.

It became necessary to come back to reality. The Church lobby wasn't an appropriate place for such wishful and soul-searching thoughts. He came to ask, not to think.

Two people entered the lobby and politely asked. "May I help you find someone?"

Derek nodded. "Yes, you can. Is your bishop here tonight?"

"Yes, we'll find him for you. His office is this way."

Derek felt safe lying in the long shadows being cast from the steeple of the Church. He spent the next few nights sleeping in the darkness of the parking lot at the Church. He made arrangements for the pickup repair to be made. He was waiting for his paycheck. It was the incident that happened to him on the morning of the fifth day that convinced him it was time to leave town, time to make an attempt to make everything right somewhere else.

Officers McDaniels and Homer visually scanned the neighborhood in their patrol car for a suspect described as a white male in his forties. They saw a man who fit the description walking down Twenty-First Street, approaching the intersection of Lynview Road. McDaniels was skeptical that this particular man could be the accused. He didn't have the gait of a person that just robbed someone's house.

The officers drove past the man on foot intently observing his body language. They made a U-turn up the road to observe the back of him. Homer, being more confident than McDaniels, radioed another police car onto the scene to follow the suspect. Then he and McDaniels drove back to where the suspect was last seen leaving his pickup in the early hours of dawn.

The pickup looked like the kind of wreck that should be searched for cocaine. The stereotypes were difficult to overcome on this one. It had all the classic symptoms of a drug-infested getaway, a decoy for something lucrative.

McDaniels had to remind himself that he wasn't there for a drug bust. He was there to serve a search warrant for a stolen possession, then the drug bust. He decided to make subjective observations before he actually presented the warrant. He walked around the pickup truck, then squinted and stretched to peer through the front window. He glanced at the floor of the cab. A toolbox, greasy cloths, a large plastic drinking cup, and a thermos jug were randomly scattered on the passenger side. He didn't see any beer cans, but he was sure that the loser had some kind of a habit.

It was obvious to him that the man was living in the bed of the pickup. A thin and shallow shell provided his shelter. He planned to pick the junk heap apart and search for drugs after he finished the search for the stolen article. For sure this guy wouldn't get off scot-free.

McDaniels and Homer left the eyesore and drove back to the suspect. His gait and pace were unchanged, and no other body language sent out messages of a criminal nature.

It was time to do their duty. The officers drove a few meters in front of him and pulled over to the side of the road. They got out of the police car to approach the pedestrian. The pedestrian looked bewildered and worried.

"I have a search warrant for your vehicle. You are under arrest for breaking and entering. You have a right to remain silent…"

Derek Clayland said nothing while he was being handcuffed. He cast his eyes downward and appeared to be frightened and confused, because he was. He didn't flinch when the officers confiscated his car keys.

Derek got in the police car. The police drove him to the heap in the Church parking lot. Officer McDaniels unlocked its door. He bent over with a flashlight to look under the front seat. From under the seat he pulled out leather bound books: the Book of Mormon, the Doctrine and Covenants, and the Bible. The spines of the books were torn and loosened from the back and front covers. He hastily thumbed through the pages. Upon the pages were red, blue, black and green ink lines with asterisks and notations marked on the edges of the pages squeezed between the lines and verses. He turned to the front of the books to see if there was someone's name claiming ownership. Each book was signed, "Derek H. Clayland."

Derek stammered, "Please tell me why I'm being arrested. What did I do? I have permission from this Church to temporarily stay on this parking lot."

McDaniels looked up from the tattered books and directly into Derek's eyes as if to send him the message, "You better listen to what I'm telling you."

"One of the residents of this neighborhood has identified you as the suspect in the robbery of her home. She claims she saw you flee the scene when she came home from her job early this morning. We have to take you into custody and book you for suspicion of breaking and entering. She'll be in to identify you from the line-up."

Derek sat silently in the back seat of the police car and waited for the officers to finish searching his pickup. He decided that it was best for him to offer the least resistance possible. His thoughts were dominated by images of himself wasting away in a horrifying prison cell. He saw himself afraid, alone, and robbed of hope. Hope had been his only salvation through these difficult times. His worst fear was not being able to prove his innocence, and then being forced to live the life of a common criminal. He feared that his name would permanently be upon criminal records that might deplete any chances of obtaining a good job.

He thought of his current job. He needed to make a phone call to the school's principal and let him know that he wouldn't be able to come in and substitute teach for the day. He had been subbing at a nearby high school. He was walking on his way to work when the police car drove up. He dreaded missing the work. He had been on a steady roll for over two weeks and was up to long-term status which almost doubled the pay. When he was through resolving the mess he was in, he would have to go back to day one. It meant building up two more weeks to obtain the long-term status again.

He decided that it should be the least of his worries. For now he needed to concentrate on convincing the law enforcers that they had the wrong guy. He hoped that the absence of a criminal record on his part would suggest that a man in his late forties wouldn't suddenly engage in a life of crime. He hoped the officers would hurry so that he could let the school know of his absence for the day.

He heard the sound of an approaching car; he glanced out the window. Behind the steering wheel he saw a distorted face tilted in anger. "*This must be the accuser who has come to accost the accused,*" he thought. He took a deep breath for a moment, and got ready for the verbal attack.

The raging woman drove up to the police car and wagged her finger at Clayland. "That's him. He did it." Her tongue lashed out obscenities. Derek said nothing in his defense.

"He's the one," the woman screeched. "He's the one that broke into my house and took my Camcorder."

"Ma'am, are you sure? We've searched his belongings. We haven't come across your Camcorder."

"But I saw him. He's the one that took my camera. He would have taken more if I hadn't walked in the house when I did. Anyway, tell him that this isn't Skid Row Alley. Tell him to take that metal carcass somewhere else, like to the dump. Tell the loser to find another place to sleep. No one wants him around here. We have a right to keep our neighborhood safe and free from scumbags who freeload off the streets. Our property values are at stake. Tell him that no one wants him around here."

"Lady, calm down," Homer said. "Meet us at the police station. We're taking him and booking him down there."

Derek maintained his silence while they drove to the police station. He began to see the picture. The accuser knew the truth. The truth was that he never broke into her place, and he never took anything. The woman would have liked it if he had. It would have given her the opportunity to shoot him. This was a ploy to get him to leave, a convincing invitation to get lost.

He arrived at the station cuffed like a common criminal. He was photographed, finger-printed, and sent into the room to be questioned. The clerk entered his social security number into the computer. He was glad that he didn't have a former police record. The thought made him feel more at ease.

"Why were you walking down Twenty-First Street?"

"I was walking to my job. I work as a substitute teacher at the high school nearby. May I please call the school to let them know they'll have to find someone else today?"

"Okay, but it's your only phone call."

He thought it would be best to use his only call to save his job. He didn't want to call Adriana because he knew how she would react. She would fall into a hysterical crying fit. Her tears always stabbed him in the heart. It was best that she not know about this. There wasn't any way that she could help him, and she didn't need any more turbulence in her life than what he was already giving her.

He called the principal of the school. He hoped that he would understand.

"Mr. Green, I won't be able to come in today. I'm experiencing a difficult emergency. May I come in tomorrow and continue with my assignment?"

"Sorry, I'll have to give the job to someone else. It's the policy. Check again in the morning. There might be something else for you."

The police tried to coerce Derek into confessing a crime, and they promised him a reduced sentence as a plea bargain.

Derek responded adamantly, "I will not commit perjury. There is no deal."

After spending the next three hours in the station, the authorities determined there wasn't enough evidence to keep Derek in jail. He didn't have a prior police record. The accuser backed off. Derek was released and sent out the door.

Derek walked to a gas station and located the telephone booth immediately. He made a phone call to Annabelle. He dreaded the thought of what he was going to have to do: he was going to have to ask her for more money. He needed to get his pickup fixed immediately so that he could find a better place to try his luck. Anyway, he didn't exactly like the city. His paychecks had been fair, but there were too many other things going against living and working in that particular community. Any one of his brothers or sisters was willing to help him out in emergencies. Annabelle answered her phone.

Derek had his pickup towed to a parking lot located behind a friend's business establishment. He spent the next two days repairing his engine. Being self-taught, he had become a very good auto mechanic. He just wasn't licensed to do it for a living.

He finished the repairs, got into his pickup, and got on the freeway. He approached the city where his mother was buried. He hadn't been to visit the grave-site since the time he was a child. It was a large cemetery. He didn't know if he would be able to find the grave, but he thought he should try. If he could see her grave one more time he swore he'd never go back to it. What was the purpose? Why was he doing it now? She wasn't there, only an old cold slab telling anyone who happened to pass by that she once existed on earth.

He pulled into a convenience store parking lot, got out of his pickup, and went inside to look at a map. He made a mental note after studying the map, then he got back in his pickup to find the cemetery. He didn't have any flowers for the grave.

He located the information center of the cemetery and went inside to see if there was a map he could use. He couldn't remember the name of the section where her grave was, only that it had a name from Church history. He scanned the names that identified the different sections. He found the section "Cumorah."

Derek walked to where the section began. Nothing looked familiar. He remembered his grandparents being buried on the other side of a small road from where his mother's grave was located. He could remember a fence, and trees that were approximately twenty yards beyond the grave. He paced between the flat headstones, searching for his mother's and his grandparents' graves. Where had she been laid to rest? Where were his grandparents? Why was it so hard to remember?

Dad used to take the family to the cemetery one Sunday out of every month. Before leaving home, they picked roses from the rose bed to place upon the grave. Dad always looked sad on those days. Jensine occasionally came with them to the cemetery. He could tell she preferred not being there. He remembered one time when Tom threw up all over the headstone. After that incident they didn't go as often.

He was about to give up his search when he found it. An etching of a Mormon Temple on the lower edge prompted his memory: Grace Clayland, "In Memory of a Loving Daughter, Wife, and Mother."

Derek suddenly missed his mother. Her songs came back to his head. Tears streamed down his face. It felt good to cry. He didn't care who saw him. Let them all think he was a big baby. His life was in ruins anyway.

"Mother, if I had a rose I'd give it to you." He turned away from the grave and began his search for his grandparents' headstones. He found them across the road.

He didn't think of himself as an itinerant homeless person. Homeless people were people who slept on benches of the city parks or over street vents on metropolitan sidewalks. He had more than what a lot of people had.

He had a truck bed to lie on and warm blankets to pull over him at night. His wife and children were living with relatives. What more could he ask for under the circumstances?

It was more of a necessity for him to send his paychecks home to his wife than for him to have a comfortable place to sleep. He didn't deserve more than what he had because of the fact that he had two children who were completely lost to him. His current family needed the basic necessities, and the former debts related to the recently failed businesses were always screaming at him.

He was grateful to Adriana's mother. He didn't know what he would do without her. She seemed to love being with her grandchildren. She always was a positive influence in their lives. They were safe where they were, void of street gangs, prostitutes, and drug dealers. He didn't understand why Adriana had to be so vocal in her trials. He wished she would try to control her weeping. He tried his best to be a good provider. Why did the Lord continually test him? Hadn't he been tested enough? He had gone through the death of his mother and the raising of his siblings. He had been misjudged, misunderstood, and misguided. He admitted to a few errors of judgment on his part, but the plight in their lives wasn't completely his fault. Most of the blame was held elsewhere.

"What a fool I have been, just like my old man. My brains are as empty as his."

In 1990, Derek became a Census taker. In going to the residences of those who didn't respond to the census mailings he discovered an unusual people. They were the splinter Mormon groups that embraced polygamy. They called themselves the Fundamentalists, the "orthodox" Mormons, the people who refused to bend to the pressures of society, government, or culture when it came to the doctrine of plural marriage. They also refused other changes in Church practices that were inspired by the prophets after President John Taylor. The splinter groups were not recognized by the Mormon Church, the Church of Jesus Christ of Latter-day Saints, as being members of their Church. Those who joined these groups were excommunicated from the Mormon Church of Jesus Christ of Latter-Day-Saints.

When he approached the families, they were friendly to him. They looked comfortable and relaxed, and very humble as to the ways of the world. In most instances the adults were cooperative in giving census information, but many of the people wanted to keep their personal data private. They didn't believe that the government should meddle in their family affairs. Occasionally, families invited him into their homes to teach him their doctrines. He was slightly curious but he declined.

Seventeen

The warmth of the springs, the heat of the summers and the frigid winters rotated throughout Derek's lifestyle. He became familiar with his surroundings, and he forced himself to be comfortable with them.

The abandoned pickup on the shoulder of the mid-western highway belonged to the man walking towards the setting sun. Derek walked with the gait of a man who had failed. The drivers and the passengers of speeding vehicles scanned the image of the man and his disabled truck. The man and his jalopy could have been the subjects of a documentary on indigent America. A stereotype of hasty judgment swept over the minds of the travelers and then faded in the recesses of thoughts that were not important enough to retain in their long-term memories. Derek was thirsty and could have used a good meal. He also needed a shower and a change of clothes. These kinds of things were becoming a luxury.

A town was ahead where he could find water and a much needed telephone. He knew that soon he could remove himself from the view of the highway travelers with their silent fleeting thoughts: You don't have time to help, he might be a criminal, someone else is in a better position to help than I am, and he doesn't expect me to help. These were normal reactions to the sight of any stranger.

Derek's pocket change was precious to him, so he decided the phone call should be collect. He hated to make collect calls but knew that Annabelle would understand. He was glad to be off the highway. As he walked, his steps were heavy. He pounded the sound of weariness into the ground.

He saw a gas station down the road. He didn't care about the gas. He just wanted to use the phone that would be there. The pattern of punching the buttons was burned into his memory. His finger raced over the number pad. Annabelle was literally his guardian. What would he do without Annabelle?

His guardian, his protector, and his forever angelic sister responded to the ring.

Twenty minutes later he waited in a Western Union office for the electronic transfer of money. He sat on a hard plastic chair shoved against the window. The chair brushed the Venetian window shades, causing the slats to tilt out of order.

He appeared to be non-complacent about the disrupted slats, as if his mind was reaching beyond tangible objects. His shirt was wrinkled. His face was tinted from the stubble of neglected facial hair. His shoes spoke the incriminating evidence of poverty.

A young woman was processing the money transaction. Standing behind the courtesy desk she glanced away from the computer monitor to study the suspicious looking stranger. She was a curious young woman, the kind of person that liked to scan passengers at airports and assess them.

She prepared to shift her eyes quickly if eye contact happened. She decided he was one of those kinds that make frequent use of the receiving end of technology. He had to be a man who never got his act together, a real loser who survived by begging from relatives.

The young woman walked over to her friend and co-worker. "Hey, that guy over there, what movie star does he look like? He looks like some movie star that I've seen. Oh! I know, the bad guy in the Superman movie. What's his name?"

"Gene Hackman." Her friend glanced at the tattered man. "Yeah, he does look like Gene Hackman. He'd look more like him if he wasn't hanging around a Western Union office."

They both laughed.

The electronic transfer finished.

"Mr. Clayland, may I see identification?"

Clayland took out his wallet and presented his driver's license to the Western Union employee.

"Thank you for using Western Union, Mr. Clayland."

Derek smiled. "You're welcome." A row of crooked teeth flashed at her.

The Western Union employee and her friend knew for certain that he was not Gene Hackman.

The repair was minor and took only a few hours to complete. The delay for his homecoming was only eight hours.

He settled for the night in the bed of his pickup at a rest stop on Interstate 80, approximately one hundred miles from where he had been stranded. The sign at the rest stop stated that overnight resting wasn't permitted. Where else was he supposed to rest? The fast moving sounds of the Interstate filtered through the thin fiberglass of the pickup's shell. The night air was still and dense, and trapped the heat of the day. In spite of the distractions, he slept deeply and undisturbed.

In the morning, he awakened to the unfamiliar landscape. It took him a moment to remove the cloud of sleep from his mind. Then he remembered the event that had brought him there. He had gone to Kansas City for a job interview. The experience ended up being another one of his failures at trying to recover from what seemed a lifetime of mistakes. Regrets were crashing down on him. He had so many regrets it was making him depressed. He was approaching age fifty. All he had to his name was a beat-up old pickup truck and a beat-up old résumé. They were both worthless. His family was the only thing worth living for. All the attempts to look for work had failed: interviews that didn't pan out, temp jobs that were nothing more than that, and job leads that led to dead ends. He learned to live with the waves of panic that seized him each time he failed.

You must make adjustments to your attitudes for the misfortunes that you are dealt with. Derek did just that. It became his survival technique. He knew he must endure his misfortunes. He was in the middle of nowhere trying to wake up from what he wished was a terrible nightmare. He had to go on. Decisions needed to be made right then and there in the middle of the flatlands of the country. He needed to come to grips with his future and the future of his family. He didn't know if going west was the right answer. After some intense thinking, he decided to continue going west and think about it while he traveled.

Fifty miles into the state of Iowa, he abruptly pulled the old pickup over to the shoulder and stopped the engine. He was confused, afraid, and didn't know what to do. He felt as if his survival technique was crumbling, and no more could he endure his misfortunes. What was the force that drove him in the direction he was going? What made him think he would suddenly find work in Utah and beyond it? He had been trying for the past several years to get work in the West. Except for his little family, there was nothing there but rejection. He felt psychotic.

He started the engine again and did a quick and complete turn of the wheel. The pickup spun around. Suddenly he was going eastward again. Spoke aloud to himself so that he could feel assured he was doing the right thing. *"I'm going to Northern Virginia. There's work in Northern Virginia. There's no work in Utah. I can't feed my family or give them a home if we live in Utah. I've already tried. I have a much better chance in Northern Virginia. Will I be able to provide a home in Virginia? Northern Virginia is a terribly expensive place to live. Of course, Adriana would have to work if we lived there..."*

He continued speaking loudly and angrily as if he was arguing with someone other than himself. "If I go east, I don't see how restitution is possible for the others." Derek felt the heavy weight of sorrow every time he thought of them. He hated himself for what he was doing to them. He abandoned them in life just as his mother abandoned him in death. She was much more fortunate than he, for she was not guilty like he was. His most recent family remained safe and comfortable at his mother-in-law's house in canyons. Except for Adriana's tears, life was peaceful there. There was no traffic congestion and the environment was clean. Except for the fact that there were no jobs there, the place was Utopia. He was crazy about his kids and they were crazy about him. He thanked God every day for them. He didn't get much of a chance to be with his family because he was always on the road looking for steady work while he worked minimum wage jobs.

Derek felt a little foolish after he had spoken to himself in such a cross manner. Driving into the glare of the sun, he drove about twelve miles into the flat terrain. He began to have reservations about his most recent decision. He pulled over to the shoulder of the road and slowed the pickup for another stop. He needed to do some more thinking, along with some praying. He began to cry, at first slightly, then uncontrollably. His sobs became very intense and expressive. They bounced off the metal ceiling of the cab. His wailing sounds made him thankful that he was isolated. He sobbed at his foolishness. He sobbed at his stupidity. He sobbed because he felt so helpless. He wept for all his children that he had betrayed. He wept until the sun moved over his head. In the beating heat, he shut his eyes and blanketed his emotions with the security of sleep.

He seemed to be able to think better after he awoke in the evening. He tried to imagine what his lost son and daughter looked like. He held on to hope for restitution. He hoped he would be able to make up for his neglect. He had faith that he could. He prayed that his family would forgive him, and that God would forgive him. In his mind his children grew: baby, child, teenager, adult. Except for the gradual growth of his children, he allowed their features to stay the same. His daughter, Wendy, had blue eyes and dark brown hair: soft, curly and falling upon high cheeks. Her nose complimented her eyes and gave integrity to the structure of her eyebrows. His daughter saw him and ran to him with her arms stretched out. In his imagination, she embraced him thousands of times. Together they talked about many things. They laughed together and they cried together.

Cole's features were more like his. It was easy to paint them on Cole as long as he referred to his own photo album. He allowed Cole's loose curls to fall upon his forehead, sweeping over his ears like the school picture in his own sixth grade photo. When Cole got older, his hair was thick and unmanageable, so was always kept short. He gave Cole his nose, his eyes, his chin, his color, his heart and his soul. He thought Cole might wonder what his biological father looked like, but Cole probably wasn't too interested in coming face to face with the man who furnished his genetics. He was probably one of those angry little boys that sulked because life didn't give him a fair shake. Derek hoped Cole would be like his half-sister, Wendy. In his mind, they both had a forgiving heart.

He had stolen their heritages.

The man sitting in the pickup on the shoulder of the highway looked at the horizon beyond the windshield of his metal habitat. Horizons had always encouraged him to keep going. Perhaps that was his problem to begin with. He had seen too many horizons in his lifetime. He decided he must drive on and be reunited with his little family. He would take care of them and continue to hope.

Eighteen

In defense of his self-esteem, Derek long ago decided that appearances were not important to him. The pickup and its shell had been dented as a result of a minor traffic mishap. He patched it the best he could then gave the metal a new coating of spray paint. The color turned out to have more orange than the red on the paint can indicated. He preferred less orange, but he kept it as it was. He blamed society for not having accepted orange as a color for vehicles. He justified the impropriety of the hue by convincing himself that he would be more visible to other drivers.

He had come to accept his lifestyle. He once had a goal of building a house in the canyon. He once had a goal of having partial custody of his other two children. He could see them vividly in his imagination, encompassed in the folds of his family. Wendy would sleep in Mariah's room and Cole in Andrew's room. And they'd all be together, enjoying each other's company as family. He stretched his imagination to include a hearth, a country kitchen like the one his mother had wished for, and a cozy cushioned rocking chair with a cat purring by the fire. There would be no fighting or quarreling with each other. But most of all he would be their father for a little while. There would be a special bond between them. He had come to accept the fact that it would happen only in his imagination.

He was feeling the eternal effects of his lingering stupidity. His sojourn on earth was turning out to be a disaster. It was too late to turn back and make all the right decisions. He had to put too many other people in front of himself. Between the laws of the land and the doctrines of the Church he had no personal privileges and freedoms left. He was bound by his mounting responsibilities. He was ridden with guilt for his failures to fulfill them.

Often he thought of the reasons why life hadn't given him a fair shake. His psychologist had analyzed his situation accurately. He was convinced that his chronic failures were attributed to his mother's actions. Her last request was for him to take care of his brothers and sisters. The next time he saw her she was lying in a coffin prepared to be lowered into the earth. He was only six years old. He was too young to take care of his brothers and sisters. What did she expect? He was only a little child. He had tried to fulfill his mother's last request, but taking care of his brothers and sisters was a very difficult task. He could remember feeling like he had failed in his duties. In the past, he and Jensine had had serious conflicts. He could remember how she had tried to exert parental authority. He hadn't wanted to allow it. Now he could see how he was wrong to interfere. He not only failed at fulfilling his mother's last request, he failed at being a good son. Perhaps being a failure in his childhood was the reason why he was such a chronic loser in adulthood. He missed his mother so much he could hardly stand it. Why did she have to die? Didn't God know that he and his brothers and sisters needed her? They all had the right to grow up with their mother.

He often thought of things that his mother could have spoken the last time he saw her. He wished she had said, "Derek, don't grieve for me. Be a happy little boy. I entrust someone else to your care and keeping. Go on with your life, and be the best that you can be. I give you to someone else to love you and nurture you, for I have no other choice." If only Dad had stopped in the hallway for a few minutes. She could have said the right dying words to him.

Derek's thoughts often went back to his mother's funeral as well. He was at the grave-site with his family. They were walking away from the grave. He stopped and turned around. He didn't want to leave her like that. The casket was still there. She wasn't in the ground yet. Someone might take her away. Her death wasn't final until she was in the ground. His family wouldn't let him stay to watch her go down.

Dad had messed him up, too. He had been as dense as they come. He made a lot of stupid mistakes since the time Mother died, one mistake after another; even falling for a scam or two when trying to find a wife. Dad's mistakes affected him. What did Dad expect? And as far as searching for a wife: did he think some woman would just waltz into his life and replace his children's mother, and everything would be fine, and that family life would be wonderful and normal? The genealogical research his father had involved himself in showed his stupidity. Researching the names of dead ancestors? His father had more important things to do than to research dead ancestors. When they had lived at the raisin farm, Dad often came into his room before the crack of dawn to shake him awake. "It's time to wake up, Derek. The Alvord line needs to be worked on." Did Dad really think he should actually get up before the crack of dawn and work on genealogy? Derek wished he'd had a normal Dad. Fathers were supposed to play ball with their sons, not obsess themselves with dead relatives. He couldn't remember a time when his father ever played ball with him.

He decided that his father had always been a poor example to him. Dad dropped out of college, never explaining the reason. He ended up being a loser of a raisin farmer. He believed his father was another reason why he, as Henry's son, was such a chronic loser. Henry was probably more to blame than Grace was for the way their son's life turned out. He used to think of Jensine as a wicked stepmother. Now he could see how wrong he was. He felt terrible for all the times he was so mean to her. She was basically a good person. She had a lot of faith. She must have gone through a lot of trials living with Dad. Any other woman would have left the marriage in its early stages. Dad took advantage of Jensine from the very beginning. He married her so he could have a full-time babysitter. His intentions were totally screwed up. He had been a bad example. Because of Dad's bad example, Derek was denied the privilege of being a good provider and a father to his own children. Henry Clayland, his father, would answer for that before the Lord.

Derek diverted his thoughts as he approached the state of Ohio. I had been living in Ohio so, naturally, Derek planned on swinging by to visit me and my family. I arrived home early from a class that evening. I was surprised to see the notorious orange pickup truck parked in front of my house. I had seen it once before. I walked in the house and there was Derek! It was a pleasant surprise to see him. After a hug, Derek and I settled down for an intense visit. My kids and their dad were watching television in the next room.

"Derek, how have you been?"

He forced a smile. "I'm trying to survive."

"Aren't you always? Where's your family?"

"They're still in Utah."

"Still living with Adriana's mother?"

Derek sighed, "Yeah."

"Where are you looking for work?"

"All over. I'm trying to stay in the west."

"Well, there isn't any work around here that I know of. You're welcome to stay here and look."

He shook his head. "Thanks, but I need to go on in the morning."

I paused for a moment and then frowned. "What happened to the mold and trim business you and Jack were doing? I heard you were doing well. Someone told me that you had a whole crew working for you, and that production was going great. You had a factory, tools, employees, and raw material. I thought your product was in big demand."

Derek smiled bitterly. "Jack and I were doing great. We had contracts lined up. As contractors, you have to pay the employees before you can pay yourself: taxes, benefits, insurances. One day I discovered that the payroll was missing."

"What happened?"

"Jack wiped out the bank account to open a restaurant in Ogden. He claims he was only borrowing the money. He said he was going to replace it but he was never able to."

"How much did he take?"

His voice dragged. "You don't want to know, but it was enough to ruin me."

I felt that Derek wanted to change the subject, but I wanted to know what happened next. "What did you do about it? Did you try to get the money back, sue him, or accuse him, or somehow make him accountable?"

"His enterprise was a big flop. We sold the business to pay the employees and some of the debts, but I still ended up in bankruptcy. Jack was sorry that he took the money without my consent. I lost so much. It was a stupid thing to do in the first place."

"You must have been furious."

His voice mellowed. "I was at first, but I've forgiven him."

"If it had been me I wouldn't have. Get a lawyer. He betrayed you."

Derek spoke defensively. "He has nothing, just as I have nothing. I've forgiven him for what he did. It's a commandment to forgive those who offend you and harm you. It's in the past now. Let's not talk about him anymore."

"Sure."

"Well, after that I did the census for a while. I ran into some interesting people there in Utah. I didn't make much. It was just another job to get me and the kids and Adriana by for a while."

There was another long pause between us. I broke the silence. "If you had it to do over again what would you have done differently?"

"I've made a lot of stupid mistakes in my life. I can't seem to undo them. I'm into my fifties now, and I have nothing. I've never owned a house, never had any money. I never made any smart moves."

"You have two little kids that are crazy about you."

"They're all I have. I seem to be losing Adriana. She gets mad at me all the time. She's either mad or she's sad. Or she's mad and she's sad. I'm a failure and she reminds me of it. She doesn't say anything, but I feel it"

"I think you would have made a good FBI agent. Or an astronomer, or some kind of researcher."

"I sure didn't play my cards right, just like Dad. He always was a bad influence on me."

I frowned. I didn't like the way the conversation was going. "So, you're going to blame Daddy for the wrong decisions you've made?"

Derek's voice became a bit confrontational. "Yeah, he was pretty stupid. He bought a raisin farm. Of all the farms to buy, why did it have to be a raisin farm?"

"Think of all the lessons we learned," I responded.

"Like what? You tell me one lesson that we learned from the raisin farm."

It was difficult to think of one, but I knew there had to be an answer. I thought for a few seconds. Then the perfect answer came to me. "Well, I have never complained about the price of raisins." I decided to quickly change the subject. "How often do you see Wendy and Cole?"

Derek's countenance grew dimmer. A despondent look came across his face. He quickly tried to cover it but I noticed it instantly. I needed to make him feel at ease.

"We can talk about something else," I said.

"Yes, I'd rather. I'll just say that Marlene won't let me see Cole. Adriana and I tried to get some custody of him. And I know that Wendy has no interest in seeing me. Please don't make me talk about them."

I tried to steer the conversation towards the positive and discuss things of interest. I knew he liked research. We talked about research.

"The research you won't see me doing is genealogy."

"Why, what's wrong with doing genealogy?"

"Because of the old grape farmer we had as a father. It was wrong of him to be so involved in genealogy."

I defended my father and his hobby. "It was a worthy cause, and I think it made him feel better about himself."

Derek was ready with his reply. "It wasn't a worthy cause, and he had better things to do with his time. His 'worthy hobby' took him away from what he should have been doing all along, like taking better care of his kids. You weren't there on those cold mornings in the boys' room. In the middle of the winter he'd come bursting in when I was fast asleep. I'm talking five in the morning. He would order me to get out of bed and work on the Alvord line. Work on genealogy at five in the morning? Who in their right mind would do genealogy at five in the morning? He had no right to tell me to, it should have been my choice to do it."

When he said that, I decided that Derek's sense of humor had, at some point in his life, shifted into the same gear as his honor and integrity. "Derek, don't you remember that we used to laugh about it? It was Daddy's way of telling you to get out of bed, go out to the barn and milk the cow."

"Genealogy, raisins, it's all worthless stuff because we did nothing but suffer. Dad didn't deserve my mother. She was so much smarter than he ever was."

"Well, you surely didn't think that about him when you spoke at his funeral. You practically assigned him the same status as the prophets. He's been dead all these years, so now you've changed your mind about him? Why Derek? What happened to your tender heart? Daddy loved you, he loved all of us. Did he ever tell you about the social services coming after him? He told me about it. They told him he wasn't a fit parent, and that he'd better find someone who could take care of us or they would. He told me that he so badly wanted us to stay together. He was willing to do anything to keep us together. How many men would do that? He did what he thought was right. He didn't run away from his responsibilities. He handled it in the way he thought was right. I loved my father, and I don't like you saying negative stuff about him."

"Well, he never played ball with me."

I stopped in my tracks. "So that makes him a bad…"

"Let's talk about something else." Derek was tired of arguing and so was I.

Another long pause revealed the mood of the dismal dialogue. "What are your plans now that the census is over?"

"I'm going back westward. I'll keep looking for work. There's some industry relocating from Southern California. I'll work for a temp agency for a while until something permanent opens. Did I tell you that I came close to getting a teaching job in California? I had an interview, but I didn't get the job. Some young guy got it."

I think he was trying to make me feel sorry for him. I wished I could make his pain go away. He seemed such a beaten man. He should have stepped into a good career long ago like my husband did, and stuck with it. Learn, grow, and continually improve job skills was the name of the game. I wished someone would have taught Derek that. Dad probably didn't because Dad probably didn't know it. He came from a different kind of generation.

Jensine wouldn't have taught him either because Derek wouldn't have let her teach him anything. If Jensine told him something he would have done the opposite. If she told him to not get higher education, to not specialize in a field of study, to not build on it, and to not take continuing education, he would have done the opposite, and he would not be sitting before me looking as though he was taking a violent beating from the world around him.

"I'm sorry to hear that. Have you tried looking into the schools in Arizona? There are probably more bilingual people there than in Utah. With your fluency in Spanish you should be able to find something."

"I've looked, yes. I've looked everywhere, it seems, from the Pacific Ocean all the way to New York City."

I thought for a minute. "What about computer jobs? Aren't there computer jobs in Utah or California?"

"Most industries hire young people fresh out of college. They usually end up hiring their interns."

"That makes a lot of sense to me. Please don't give up, Derek, not every industry out there thinks that fifty-year old people don't have any brains."

"Let's talk about something else."

I couldn't think of very many topics that would please him. The only topics of conversation I could think of were destined to be devastating. As long as we were on the roll I decided to ask him the big one: the one that would stir up his concealed emotions. "What do you think about the theory that our mother really died because she was anorexic?"

Derek seemed surprised that the issue was addressed and he responded quickly. "It makes me furious. I hope you don't think she was anorexic, because it isn't true."

"Oh, I don't know, Derek. You know you might be wrong. It's a hard thing to deal with. They're saying that your mother died because of a mental illness when all this time she was supposed to be perfect. Both Uncle Samuel and Uncle Edwin are adamant that she was anorexic. Who knew her better than her brothers? I don't want to believe it any more than you do, but we can't believe just what we want to believe. Truth isn't whatever you want it to be, Derek." He wasn't listening. He was determined to convince me.

"She didn't die of anorexia. I can't believe that anyone would even suggest it."

I got up to check on the kids. Derek was left alone with his thoughts, and I with mine. Sarcasm chimed in my head: *All right, Derek, have it your way. Truth is assimilated then conveniently tailored to your comfort. Our mother didn't have anorexia because she was too perfect to be suffering from a psychological disease. This means we'll have to go to the cemetery and tear up Dad's headstone and toss it away. We'll have to get a new headstone, with a new inscription that reads: "SOME OF US ARE GLAD WE CAME TO LIVE WITH YOU."*

Nineteen

In her younger days, Alice Madison had the face and body of a beauty queen. When people saw this beautiful cousin of ours it was difficult for them to not affix their gaze longer than the norms of society allowed. The girls studied her long enough to envy the structure of her brow and the way her mouth curved into shapely lips. Her deep blue eyes sparkled under the shade of the thin eyebrows that she penciled in to accentuate her eyes. Black curly hair brought an added softness to the olive tone of her face.

She was a woman who placed her trust in the healing powers of nature. She believed that all healing was rooted in the resources of the earth. The bookshelves in her home held volumes on theories and techniques of herbal healing. She learned the theories of the masters, and actively practiced their applications. She kept her home potted with several Aloe Vera plants in order to conveniently access the miraculous pulps when the occasion called for it. The long green prickly arms of the plant, plump with the juices of healing, made a pleasant contribution to the atmosphere of her home. In her opinion, the Aloe Vera plants lost their proper spirit when she discovered that a commercialization of the plant appeared on the market shelves in the form of soaps, lotions, shampoos, and tonics. She continued the upkeep of her plants despite the insult to their reputation as a mysterious healer. She shared her knowledge of the healing powers with her friends. She was able to convince them that the content was a cure-all for any skin ailment, particularly burns; and taken internally, it was a grand nutrient.

She felt that procreating was a sacred duty of all women bonded in marriage. She had eleven sons and daughters, and several grandchildren accredited to her posterity. She believed that childbirth was a natural act to be reserved for the confines of the home, without anesthesia or delivery tables. She often assisted the local midwife with home births. She helped to instruct the men on how to assist in relieving the excruciating pains of childbirth as their women would squat in labor, working with the law of gravity to bring the children downward into mortality.

She had little tolerance for metropolitan cities. She had tried her hand with them years earlier and had been miserable. The pace of living annoyed her. She felt claustrophobic. She took advantage of the first opportunity that became available to move back to a small town.

When her husband was at work, Alice stayed busy with her domestic responsibilities. She made her home comfortable yet practical. Separate living quarters within her home provided a place for her mother, Jane. Jane, another sister of Grace's, was the closest sibling to her in age. Aunt Jane had a delightful personality and a talent for being able to turn any dull story into a most exciting adventure for any listener. She had two woeful marriages behind her. Alice had few memories of her alcoholic father, who had abandoned them when she was very young. And her stepfather was a tarnished man by his own actions.

Alice was involved in the Young Women's Organization at Church. As she became acquainted with the girls, she noticed that many of them were becoming indoctrinated to the ways of the world. The young Mormon women were selecting male dominated careers to go into: medicine, dentistry, law, and engineering. She felt that these careers were not becoming to Mormon women. She admitted that she had old-fashioned values, but they were values that she believed were sanctioned by the Lord.

She was a devoted mother to her children and a dutiful homemaker. Her wheat mill was the most important appliance in her kitchen. She fed her family cracked wheat cereal for breakfast each morning. Her frugal resources were a benefit to the pocketbook as well as a boon to the health of her children.

Alice loved going to Church. Her husband sat on the High Councils for a number of years. They both taught lessons and served in leadership positions in each of the Church's auxiliaries. But in her middle age, she began to have a difficult time attending the Relief Society meetings. She wasn't agreeing with some of the policies and practices of the women's auxiliary. She began to scoff at the sign-up sheets that were passed around for the mini-class workshops. In her opinion, frivolous and unnecessary lessons were being taught. The making of craft items for the decor of the home was not necessary to the sustainment of life. She believed that only the basics of living should be taught. If anyone had asked her to teach a class in herbal remedies, she would have been willing. She knew that the Church leaders wouldn't approve of such a class.

She found herself becoming increasingly irritable with the Church leaders. They were losing touch with reality. They were all becoming caught up with the "ways of the world."

In her quest to make sense of her new way of thinking, she began to seek alternatives to her Mormon religion.

Twenty

In 1996 Derek and his family were living in a small two-bedroom apartment in Tooele. He was self-employed as an auto detailer, making just enough to pay the rent and put a little bit of food upon the table. After living with her mother for several years, Adriana finally had a home that she and the children could call their own. As much as she loved her mother, Adriana needed her own place. Although the neighborhood was undesirable and the apartment was crowded, it was theirs. Water leaked into their shower from the apartment located above theirs, there was no washer and dryer connection, and the apartment wasn't air-conditioned. An absence of window screens made it so they didn't even have the breeze of the cool night air to make them feel comfortable. In spite of the fact they were renting, it was their own home.

I booked a passage on a flight to Salt Lake City, due to arrive on a Saturday afternoon, Memorial Day weekend. The quick trip was to help my daughter relocate to a different university. My plan was to rent a vehicle large enough to make it possible. On the plane the stewardess demonstrated how, in an emergency situation where the cabin is deprived of oxygen, you must put an oxygen mask on yourself before you put one on your child. In other words, you must be able to preserve yourself before you can preserve someone else.

I called Derek on the phone and let him know I would be in town. I asked him if we could get together for an hour or two, perhaps over lunch, before I took off northward bound. When I explained the reason for my trip, Derek offered to drive me to the city of my destination. But I was concerned for my brother. His only crime in the world was that he was always poor, destitute, and desperate. I felt my place in his life should be at the rock-bottom of his priorities.

"Don't you work on Saturdays?" I didn't want to take him away from any kind of obligation to his family.

"Not this Saturday. Adriana and the kids are going to her mother's for the weekend. I'll get to spend some time with you."

In spite of my feeling of guilt, I accepted his offer. "Well, okay. But if you need to work or be with your family just let me know."

Derek marked his calendar.

Two-thousand miles to the east a statue named Serenity remained in her sorrowful state, waiting for more destruction to happen.

The plane was crowded, as were my goals. I had a conversation with two young Mormon missionaries who got on the plane in Saint Louis. The clean-cut young men revealed that they were returning from the South African mission. I told them about my father's desire to wrangle stories out of the old South African settlers in 1927 when he was a Mormon missionary. I told them I have a notebook full of interesting stories and legends of

South Africa as told by those he had encountered. The plane touched down.

After disembarking the plane, I saw Derek waiting by the baggage claim. A metamorphic kind of change had come over him, the kind that comes with age or stress. I'm sure he saw a change in me as well. Despite the change, he was still the Derek I had always loved. I glanced over my shoulder at the missionaries and watched them fall into the arms of their families and friends. A quick hug for Derek and a walk to the parking garage initiated our weekend together.

We got into his pickup truck and headed north towards Idaho. The air was warm and windy. The windows were open, and the traffic was loud and fierce; a redefinition of the land of my heritage. I had always thought of Utah as being cool in the spring and subdued in spirit all year round. We traveled the Interstate. Its aggressiveness reminded me of the one back at my home in Maryland.

Had my pioneer forefathers envisioned their valley would become what I saw all around me? When Brigham Young announced "This is the right place", did he know that horseless carriages of all sizes and dimensions would speed up and down the valley floor? Had they envisioned the crime and the poverty, features of any civilization that embraces the principles of freedom? Or was their vision only of a valley of refuge for the religiously oppressed migrants of the Mormon faith?

We approached the northern end of the Salt Lake valley. Derek suddenly thrust his arm out the window and swept it over the landscape, and he spoke one harsh word.

"Babylon." He spoke the word with anger and judgment in his voice.

"Babylon" was the word used to describe those who were caught up in materialistic pride. Was Derek giving a blanket judgment to the citizens of the Salt Lake Valley? It was only one word, but it alarmed me. I remained restrained and silent.

Conversation lulled between the times we had to stop to refill the leaky oil tank.

As we approached Logan, we decided it was a good time and place to stop and eat. As we dined, Derek asked me if I had ever seen the house where Mamma grew up. We knew that Mamma grew up in Logan, for she often talked about the beloved city of her family.

"I think I went there when one of Mamma's sisters married. I don't remember it though. I think I was about three because I remember a hot pink dress that I had, and I had it on when I was in a group picture at that wedding reception. So I must have been there but I just remember the hot pink dress…"

Derek interrupted my story about the dress before I dragged it on any further. "Let me take you to see her childhood home."

"Sure." I felt curious as to why Derek was interested in Mamma's childhood home. I had always assumed that Derek never thought highly enough of Mamma to be interested in anything about her. Her childhood home! "*Whatever possesses him to want to see it?*" I asked myself.

We drove to the street where Jensine lived as a child. Small sturdy brick houses lined the street. The houses were a stone-throw apart from each other, and each back yard was deep enough for the home dweller to have the option of planting fruit trees and gardens for seasonal produce.

I stared out the window. "For some reason I always thought she lived on a farm. What happened to the farm?"

"No, it's easy to assume that she was raised on a farm. That's what most people from Utah did back then: farm. There wasn't much else to do. Her dad was actually a janitor at the local school. He walked to work every day. The family walked everywhere because they didn't have a car. The churches and the stores were nearby, and the schools were in walking distance, so they really didn't need a car. I suppose that's why Mamma never learned to drive. It just wasn't necessary for her to learn."

I was surprised that Derek had some family stories about Mamma. Jensine's childhood home was in keeping with the traditions of the pioneers: use only what is necessary, don't be extravagant. Mamma had ten siblings, so they must have put a few kids in a loft. Derek wasn't positive that it was her childhood home, but he knew we were in the vicinity of it. He had only his memory to rely on. After a quick glance from out of the window of the truck, we were focused back on the main highway going north.

Evening approached. The stretch of highway lay flat on the level terrain. Trees were scarce in comparison to the forests that flourished on both sides of Interstate 95 in Maryland. The mountain ranges in the distance were a refreshing sight. It was during the trip northward that I learned that Derek had abandoned the religion in which he was nurtured and replaced it with a splinter that embraced polygamy. It was his choice and his comfort zone. He expected tolerance. He appealed to the Mormon decree on the subject of religious tolerance, the Eleventh Article of Faith: *"We claim the privilege of worshiping Almighty God according to the dictates of our own conscience, and allow all men the same privilege; let them worship how, where, or what they may."*

Derek continued with new dialogue. "I want to tell you about a dream that I had. If what I say starts to disturb you, please tell me to stop."

Dreams can crack the brain at an alarming rate, in my heartfelt opinion. But doomsday dreams were never anything I could relate to. He dreamed of fires and earthquakes. The fire in the mountains of the Wasatch wasn't anything I could even imagine. I liked things as they were. Earthquakes, thunders, storms and whirlwinds were for another time and culture as far as I was concerned. So my brother was a dooms-dayer. So what, I thought. Let him think what he wants, if that will make him happy.

We arrived safely at our destination. The evening was warm, windy, and gray. I was glad to see Beth and she was glad to see me. We spent the evening packing her things for a move. Outside the apartment, the wind whipped its sounds around throughout the evening and into the night. It was a howling kind of a wind, creeping through the cracks and rattling the thin panes in the window frames as if to send the message that no barrier is completely impermeable.

The trip back to Provo was pleasant as it should have been. Beth's laughter filled the air as she talked of friendships she had made and the fun things she had done. When our conversations lulled for a few minutes, the issues I had with my brother resurfaced, and my mood grew somber as well as my thoughts.

If he was so sold on polygamy, then Derek probably had an extra wife or two and was not confessing it. I was aware of the polygamous persuasions that were scattered throughout Utah and its neighboring states. I had read a book, <u>Prophet of Blood</u>, the story of Ervil LeBaron and his murderous clan. However, it would be unwarranted to compare the typical plural family with the LeBaron clan.

I had some knowledge of polygamy in its current and historical perspectives: Those who practice polygamy are not prosecuted by the law unless they do things like perform forced or underage marriages. The government does not honor a marriage beyond the original one and doesn't consider any others as binding and legal. But to those who honor plural marriages, that doesn't matter because, to them, the Lord sanctions it; He is the one who ultimately governs. In the early days of the Mormon Church, after the federal government passed the edict banning polygamy, law officers threw hundreds of Mormon men into prisons for continuing with their responsibilities to their families. The government found itself in an awkward and embarrassing position. Behind bars, there were no opportunities for the inmates to provide for their families.

I thought of my family history. Once I saw a picture of one of my great-great grandfather with his family of wives and his brood of kids. Families must have been expansive: dozens of little half brothers and sisters scurrying about, wives quarreling over territorial rights, and then the sleeping arrangements!

The crowded conditions of the pickup cab made it sensible for us to press forward without interruptions. The highway was scarce of vehicles in comparison with the highways of the eastern United States. The hum of the pickup's motor lulled everyone into a state of drowsiness. There seemed to be a need for dialogue, but not about religion.

In the midst of travel, topics of conversations came and went. We spoke of controversial issues of the day. His opinions and theories led me to form my own conclusions about the formation of his new lifestyle. I had taken psychology classes in college so I knew somewhat of the nature of the mind. The conclusion I came to was that Derek was no longer able to exist in the Mormon subculture: a subculture that teaches that a man's most important calling in life is to be a responsible person and to provide the necessities of life for his family. Derek had failed miserably. He no longer fit in with his faith. This man's connection with his faith became buried within the silent restraints of an irreparable past. My brother's apostasy from the Mormon faith was based on psychological and sociological motives, and it had nothing to do with religion. Sitting beside me was a man who had become an outcast of society. He once belonged to the American society that viewed financially non-supportive fathers as being criminals. Its customs and policies were construed to deny him the right to participate in the nurturing of his children. His mission slipped away from him, all because of money.

In his former society, the laws of the land didn't allow him to share custody of his children without the interference of monetary regulations. In his adulthood, Derek became the victim of the same injustice experienced by his father: social opinion that a man isn't capable of nurturing his children. Derek was the prey of a society that equates child support with money and a social system that puts price tags on children. His new society was one in which he was able to survive. A son and daughter became lost to him in a blinding fog. He tried to reach out in the fog, hoping for its density to lift. He hoped to find their hands, their hearts, and their souls. But the fog remained fixed, connected to the earth: bound, uncaring, unforgiving, and uncompromising. His first-born child was soon to become an adult. His second child was a teenager. These children would never know, feel, or be part of the love and the heritage that their father could have offered them.

I thought of our parents. How sad they would have been to claim their grandchildren only in their thoughts. These were mortal beings of their flesh, who they were not entitled to be with on earth. I thought of how this situation must be widespread throughout society. How many people have children or grandchildren that they have been denied: empty names written on a family group sheet, or despairing thoughts written on the pages of a journal? How many children hear the degradations that are spoken from the mouths of their mothers each time the fathers miss payments of child support or are late with them? Share the children with the fathers, and don't make money the weapon that kills relationships.

Derek was pulled into the polygamous cult by the welcoming embraces of someone who was familiar to him. Our cousin Alice Madison, who had apostatized from the Mormon religion, invited him to the meetings. I never blamed Alice for my brother's decision to join the society, embrace polygamy, and continue to multiply and replenish the earth. It was bound to have happened. In my opinion, his preparation for it began the first day he missed payments of child support. That day was the day he began his downfall from serenity and Serenity. His lack of money denied him from nurturing, caring, and participating in the lives of his children. Money manipulated him out of his God-given right to be a father to his children. That was the day Derek began his descent from society and the Mormon subculture.

He now belonged to a society in which he was accepted and loved unconditionally. The people didn't ostracize him as his former acquaintances had. They didn't reap upon him the same stigma that social services placed upon those who weren't financially supportive of their children. They didn't criticize and judge him harshly because he wasn't able to give his family all that they wanted and needed. The people welcomed him with loving arms and they held him in high esteem. They made him become important to them and their cause. They extended their friendships unselfishly. No more arrests for crimes he didn't commit. He was safe and secure in a communal living situation, living a form of the United Order. It was a principle that had been practiced by the early Mormon pioneers. Separated from their federal government's economic institutions, the pioneers lived a higher law that provided assistance to the poor and the destitute saints of the Church. Property, money, and goods-in-kind had been pooled so that the poor and the needy Church members could feed their families. Those who were not able to work were blessed by those who were. Those who made sacrifices received blessings from the Lord. In the early days of the Church, the United Order was discontinued when many of the saints were no longer willing to live the principles of it.

We were almost in Utah.

Twenty-One

After Derek dropped Beth and me off at the motel in Provo, he drove to the city of his friends. That weekend, as Adriana tucked the children into bed at their little home in Tooele, Derek entered into doctrine of polygamy. Driven by his new-found religious beliefs, without the knowledge and consent of his wife, he took another wife by definition of his religion. He justified his action by reasoning that the Lord had commanded him to take another wife.

Two weeks after his illegal marriage, Derek mustered the courage to tell Adriana what he had done. He called her at her mother's home. She had been staying there because he was no longer coming home at night, and the kids were out of school for the summer.

On the phone he told her quickly. Her silence was violent. Her heart beat wildly.

"How could you? When did you do it?"

Derek responded meekly. "Two weeks ago."

"I was gone but I came back on Monday."

"Yeah."

"That was the evening I drove all the way to Provo to pick up Camilla at the car rental because you said you had to work. That was the night I fixed a special dinner for us because she was leaving early in the morning. We waited three hours for you to at least call us. You didn't show up until one in the morning—because, I suppose, you were on a honeymoon!"

"Yeah, Adriana, but I was supposed to...."

Adriana interrupted. "So you're saying you lied to me. While you were off committing adultery, I was waiting at home for you to come home and be with your family!"

"I wasn't committing adultery. I was getting married because I was supposed to. The Lord commanded me to."

"So you got married on Monday night to someone, and then came home at one in the morning to be with me, your real wife. Derek, that's crazy! You're nothing by a big cheater. Whoever it is that you married is your mistress, not your wife. You have really hurt me and your children."

Derek didn't defend himself. He allowed Adriana to continue to let off steam. "You married me! Anyway, I thought I was supposed to approve of your taking another wife!"

When polygamy was practiced in the early days of the Church it was necessary for a man to have the approval of his first wife before he was allowed to take additional wives.

She tried to control her voice and not weep as she had done hundreds of times before. "You never asked me. You knew what I'd say, and how I'd feel. How could you do this to us?"

She waited for the final words that would slay her marriage. There were only four of them.

"You're still my wife."

When he said it, fury raged inside her. The skin on her face vented the heat. "Not anymore." She slammed down the receiver.

Adriana sunk into despair. She was deeply wounded. She had thought she would never give up on her husband of twelve years. She had been determined to support him, to stand by him through the thick and the thin, to be long-suffering through all her tears and the tears of the children. She had even stayed with him when he left their Mormon religion and fell into his polygamous religion. She tolerated it but she had warned him, "If you pay tithes to your Church, if you try to indoctrinate the children, if you take another wife, if you do any one of these I'll leave you and take the children with me."

Adriana thought of the many lonely nights without Derek. She began to feel the effects of a wound that spread to the edges of her soul. The anger turned to hurt and she cried. But within her sorrow, she felt a sense of comfort. In the haste of her anguish, in the stream of her tears, a reassurance fell upon her. She suddenly realized that she had a valid reason for ending her unhinged marriage. As she pondered her new trial, she realized her future might now be hopeful. She began to look forward to a sense of security for herself and for her children.

Adriana dried her tears. She should have known what was going on in his mind. The Monday after Memorial Day, she arrived back in Tooele with the children. She noticed a few things were missing. She didn't try to understand the reason. She noticed that his coat wasn't in the closet when it wasn't the right season to wear a coat. At the time, she hadn't thought to reason why it was gone. How blind she had been! He had basically already abandoned her and the children, a premeditated abandonment. Items gone and no note with explanations should have made the situation obvious. Now it was time for her to face it.

Adriana's mind churned with pain, despair, gladness, peace, insecurity, and anger; but within the mixture of her emotions a ray of hope enveloped her. The feeling warmed her. No longer would she have to lie awake at night wondering where he was: Was he safe? Had he eaten a good meal? Where was he? When would he return to them? No longer would her eyes fill with tears when he called her on the telephone to report his status of searching for work. No longer would she suffer the embarrassment of dire poverty, homelessness, and economic ruin. She began to make her plan of action.

She planned on turning to the welfare system to seek help. She heard of "Displaced Homemakers," a program that helped women in domestic plights. Possibly they could assist her in finding a place to live, and in finding employment. It was about time that she got her own place, her own life. It was time she reclaimed her self-esteem.

She was still mad at Derek's cousin Alice for inviting him to the cult meetings. After Derek had gone a few times, she had begun to notice a change in him. His phone calls were fewer. He became distant with the kids. He criticized them for wanting to watch television. He had developed friendships that were strange, from her line of thinking. He talked of his new friends and tried to persuade her to enter his circles of friendship. She didn't want anything to do with them. His conversations with her seemed to be forced and artificial. They didn't argue. They quit paying attention to each other. He lost his affection towards her. Now it was all in the past. She remembered her marriage as it was in the beginning, when they had goals that they were determined to achieve together. It was a time when he was agreeable, and it was a time when she was agreeable. She knew she needed to be strong.

Once Adriana made her decision to leave Derek, she took upon new worries. Now that her husband was estranged, a sense of alarm swept through her mind. She had the children to protect. Never in her wildest imaginations had she ever thought she would fear Derek. He had once been kind, caring, and gentle. He had loved the children tenderly. She suddenly wept for the past, the way he used to be, and the way they used to be. Once again, she dried her tears. In her instincts to protect her children, things that Derek recently said to her took on different implications.

"Mariah and Andrew are a chosen son and daughter of God."

When he had said it, she had been slightly disturbed. At the time, she guessed that it was something that any doting parent would say in reference to his children. Now it shifted into a new context, into a dimension that was foreign to her culture and her religion. It was necessary to begin the divorce immediately. Her thoughts continued to be diverted to the safety of the children. She had to put them first at all costs.

"If he thinks his children are choice sons and daughters of God, it means he will want to nourish them with strange doctrines. He will want to take them away from me." She said it in her head quietly, and she said it in a prayer to the Lord out loud. She would leave her mother's home and the home they had made with each other, and escape with the children. Derek must not find them.

I arrived back at my home in Maryland without incident. My spirit was subdued from the surprising events of the week. I wondered if things might get worse before they got better. I was concerned that my brother might be caught up in a violent group such as the LeBaron clan. Although Derek assured me that violence was counterproductive to their cause, I was still concerned, and I feared that something alarming might happen. Derek's motives seemed to be based on a chronic path of failure that began with the death of our mother. His religious choice was the way to a comfortable method of thinking and acting, suitably tailored to the individual.

Since the time he was six years old, Derek followed the example of his mother in regards to the dreams of his sleep. She was a dreamer too. It seemed that Derek's dream of the dying people of the Salt Lake Valley didn't allow flexibility in concepts of cause and effect. To him there was one cause and one effect, and his dreams were as real as reality itself. His brain produced for him the scenario for the end of the world: drought, starvation and death. His new religion dictated fear and doom. The nighttime conquered his mind and his spirit. His dreams had become the master of his destiny. Selected dreams, filtered through electrical impulses, became messages from the dark.

I called my brother Tom on the phone. After chatting about frivolous stuff for a while, I asked him if Derek ever told him about his visit to the psychologist. Tom told me he hadn't.

"He told me and Annette about some sessions he had with a psychologist," I said. "We were in the car with him driving somewhere and, out of the blue, he started to tell us about a visit he had with a psychologist. I've never forgotten it. Annette says she remembers it too. Do you want to hear about it?"

"Of course I do. Go ahead."

I proceeded with the conversation. "Well, Derek went to a psychologist around the time Daddy died. His marriage to his second wife had just ended. I never even got to meet her. We live so far away. Did you meet her? Anyway, this is what happened…"

After I finished telling Tom everything that Derek had told me, he lamented: "No, it didn't happen that way. Mother didn't say it to him. She said it to me. She looked at me and she told me to take care of my brothers and sisters. She didn't say it to him."

Tom remembered the incident clearly and he described his reaction. "I didn't know that she wouldn't come back. She had been carried away before, but she always came back. There was no reason to believe she wouldn't come back again."

The conversation ended. Tom took the next several minutes to contemplate what I had told him.

Twenty-Two

The knowledge of my mother and the memories of my family that had receded into the complexities of my past could no longer be avoided. My brother's actions brought them to the surface. I began to search my past and open it up to undiscovered knowledge. I opened a box that I had stored in a closet in my home, a box that held my history, the history I had shunned for much of my life. I hoped for new discoveries that might await me.

I read letters and diaries. I read the journal entries written by my father describing my parents' romance at a statue named Serenity. The day before the wedding: August 10, 1934. *Sweetheart: We had a very enjoyable walk and talk tonight. Afterwards we went over and sat at the feet of old Serenity in Euclid Park. Remember, dear, I bought you a bouquet of gladiolas as a token of my love.* Descriptions of their love growing at Serenity's feet brought tears to my eyes because of vistas that were denied me.

I looked at a map of Washington D.C. to find where the park was located. The legend on the map indicated that Serenity was a national monument. Her home was at Meridian Hill Park, in Washington D.C. I looked through my collection of family photographs and found a picture of my mother standing against a tall and bulky gate-post. The caption on the photograph recorded the scene for Henry and Grace's posterity. "Grace at Euclid Park, 1934." I looked at the map again. Euclid Street was the street that went east and west at the northern rim of the park. The picture had to be Meridian Hill Park! The park was located across the street and down a ways from the Church. I was familiar with the Church building because I had once attended it. The Church was built of sturdy stone and the sweat of the depression era. Its architecture reflected love and devotion to a higher being, and the Angel Moroni stood triumphantly on top of its spire. The golden angel was just art to motorists passing by, who didn't quite understand it. To those who patronized the Church, it was about the teachings that were meaningful to them. For forty years, the angel cast a lot of shadows around. The angel came down when the Church building sold because of shifting demographics.

My mind flashed to the nineteen-thirties. The smell of gladiolas was in the air. My mother and father were at the feet of Serenity. How she looked, I did not know. I saw my mother rest her head on my father's strong shoulder. I was familiar with his shoulder. When I was a child it was the same shoulder I always laid my head on in Sacrament service each Sunday. I was always possessive of my position next to him. It was a moment of warmth from my father, my surrogate mother. I saw my mother and father speak affectionate words in silent tones. Within fourteen years five children were born.

I didn't know what emotions would stir in me if I ever saw Serenity. I expected it would make my spirit soar. I expected beauty, serenity, and cultural refinement.

I decided to take an afternoon and drive the sixty miles from my home to the park so I could get a glimpse of her countenance and feel her serenity. I wanted to see her in all her glory. I planned the trip.

Twenty-Three

Derek Clayland was finally at peace with himself. He returned to live in the land of his inheritance. He was finished with being itinerant in cities that battered his dreams around. This was an opportunity to unite with the roots of his heritage, a chance to abandon the insanity of the past. He would avenge the tears of all those who had ever loved him.

His new home was considered a small town in comparison to the cities further south and west, but it was growing. Small influxes of new converts were flowing in. By coming together in one location, in one Zion, they were becoming unified in purpose and in strength. His great-great grandfather had founded the larger city to the north. Other ancestors settled the nearby communities. The Mormon temple, built in the early days of the Church, was located east of the city. His religion claimed the temple was theirs, for the Mormon Church had corrupted it. They waited for the day when they could possess it as their own. They didn't believe in reclaiming it violently or illegally. God had his way for them, and His promises were kept in due time.

Derek didn't worry too much about the community being tainted by money-hungry city slickers that migrated from the Sodomic cities of Nevada, California, and others. It was only a matter of time before the world would be destroyed. The Millennium's promise for peace was only a dream away. A new era was upon them. The glory of God shined in its promise to be kind. Soon Satan would no longer be able to reign terror upon the earth and destroy families. Derek knew this was the place where God wanted him. Armageddon's destruction would impose its doom upon the metropolitan valleys of the lands eastward and upon the lands westward, and it would surge its way around the world, but he and his family would be safe. Within the decade, the destruction would reign its fury upon the wicked and swallow them up into never-ending misery. The wails of suffering would resonate regret for the materialistic pride of their hearts.

His faith knew no bounds when he thought of his children safe in the folds of his arms, their weary heads pressed against his chest, groping for comfort from the fear. He saw the vision clearly: The odor of sweltering flesh mingled with the fumes of melted synthetics would be all that was left of the Wasatch Range. First there would be homelessness, suffering, and drought. Safe on his bench, he, his family, and his friends would remain safe and secure from the destruction and its aftermath.

Derek's initiatory bride was Samantha, a tenderhearted and amiable woman in her late thirties who had been widowed for several years. She had been a plural wife and was only sixteen years old when she gave birth to her son. Her deceased husband had been a distinguished leader of the Church of the First Born and became a martyr when their son was but a boy. The murder was caused by one of Ervil Lebaron's wars of rivalry. The First Born Church was a religion that had splintered from the Mormon

Church in the 1950's. Ervil LeBaron was a high official of the apostate Church. He splintered from the Mormon Religion to create his own bloodthirsty and corrupt institution under the guise of religion. Samantha's mother was numbered among Ervil LeBaron's many wives, which made Samantha one of Ervil's stepdaughters. After Ervil was captured by law enforcement officers and sent to prison, Samantha, her mother, and her brother testified against Ervil in a court of law. After doing so, they went into hiding and changed their identities.

Derek became an important official in the leadership of the cult. He didn't mind identifying it as a cult, even though the term sounded negative. His new religion had cult-like attributes. It was small, they held rites, and they were a close knit-group. He always kept within his grasp the one thing that never failed him: his set of scriptures. He kept them at his right hand. His knowledge of the scriptures quickly took him to new heights of recognition among his peers. The words in the books of scripture were profound and unwavering. He read them deeply and intellectually, he pondered and searched references and cross-references. Because of his gift of interpretation and his knowledge of doctrines, he was held in high admiration. He believed that this was proof that God had sanctioned him to live the law of polygamy so that he could "multiply and replenish the earth."

The intellect of Derek Clayland flourished, and masked his shame.

Twenty-Four

Before they had the big blow-up over the phone, Derek had tried to convince Adriana that they should relocate to a more remote part of Utah. She was against the idea. He knew that eventually she would regret not leaving the wicked valley. He couldn't understand why she wanted to stay in a big metropolitan city. The schools were crowded, gangs went rampant, and crime was running off the charts.

Adriana was always quick to argue, "I want to stay because you finally have work. It means I finally have my own place."

Salt Lake City and the adjacent towns were a nasty place to raise a family as far as he was concerned. It just wasn't worth staying there. He tried time after time to convince Adriana of the pending destruction that would reign upon the valley. It was in the air. It was only a matter of time.

Back at my home in Maryland, I kept wondering when my state of bewilderment would cease. Derek was still a sweet brother, but his sense of humor had been destroyed somewhere along the beaten path of his life. How could a smile ever exist beside a dream of doom? There would be no time for one, or room for one. For several months following the trip to Utah, my memories and knowledge of my past fell into a state of deep reflection. The slumbering grievances of my past awakened more dread in me than my family cared to have exist. I couldn't keep this confused brother out of my thoughts. It was difficult to explain it to my family without writing it on paper within the context of everything I ever felt, heard, and knew had happened. I also thought a lot about the statue Serenity, in a park only a few miles from me. She was peace, commitment, love, sacrifice, beauty undefiled. She was my history and possibly my comfort.

Early memories continued to haunt me. Derek was only trying to protect us and take care of us because our mother was dead. He thought he was doing what he was supposed to do. He thought he was being obedient to his mother. Hadn't my brother suffered enough? Didn't he have his share of suffering when his mother was swept away in his tender years?

As far as dreams went, I was curious about the intentions of the Creator. Was He not the Creator of all, even dreams? In the capacity of our clay tabernacles mingled with spirit, what is the criterion for identification of reason? Some dreams are light and tenderhearted moments under the moon and stars. They are usually the dreams that make you search your soul and decide if the message is for you alone because of a weakness you might have. Or one's dream might be identified as a goal, a purpose, or meaning in life for mortality's harsh journey. Yet there are the dreams that bombard the slumbering brain to assault integrity, redirect the moral compass, and slap adversities upon you. It's okay though, because when you awake you are relieved and thankful that it is only a dream.

I despised Derek's doomsday nightmare. When he awoke from it, he had tagged it as a vision instead of a fantasy of the night.

Twenty-Five

It was a fall Saturday. It was a good day to see and feel Serenity. I asked my children if they wanted to go to the park in Washington to see the statue. Andy was the only one interested. We brought the city map with us. One hour south on I-95 brought us to the city. It was an adventure back into time, and I looked forward to seeing the statue Serenity: my icon of hope, the protector of my heritage, and the defender of my inner peace.

We arrived at the park without incident. My perceptions immediately adjusted to the moment of nostalgic anticipation. In spite of the weather-beaten fences and gateposts, the park became hallowed ground. We parked along the street at the southern end of the park. We got out of the car to approach the entrance to the park. We climbed the wide steps at the southwest corner. I wondered if the gatepost at the edge of the stairway was the tall one that my mother was leaning against in the photograph that my father had snapped sixty-five years earlier. I wished that I had brought the photo with me to assist in the restorations of the past.

The reflecting pool at the base of the terraced water fountain made us feel relaxed, as long as we didn't glance at the polluted cisterns of water that were stationed nearby. Colorful lily pads floated on the surface with the synchronization of the sound of the flowing water from the terraced fountain above. I commended the preservation committees for their noble attempts at restoration of the grounds. In the distance, beyond the reflecting pool, two statues came into view. We hesitantly approached them. The Dante and Buchanan statues appeared weathered and neglected. It was a fair warning to us that our Serenity might have suffered as well.

We walked up the sweeping stairway, past the stone bench which artistically balconied away from the stairway. I couldn't help but wonder how many lovers once sat there to gaze at the rushing water of the terraced falls or how many proposals of commitment must have been spoken. We reached the top of the stairway and arrived at the northern section. A speaker platform that was permanently fixed for public forums interfered with a path that once was. We merely walked a different one, one that brought us near our statue. In the distance we saw a statue on the east side of a walking path, a subdued figure. I was full of fear for her. And I wasn't sure that she wanted to meet me. Then I stood before her face. *Are you my Serenity?* The name on her base affirmed it.

We were alone in the seclusion of her shadow, an intense moment to contemplate her poise and appearance. Serenity wasn't what I expected. The Serenity that was before me quickly chided the Serenity I had painted in my mind. The Serenity that had been in my thinking stood dignified, confident, beautiful and serene; and she had a look of angelic motherhood on her face. This Serenity was reclining in a relaxing pose of sadness. Her arm reached downward. The pain of losing a limb was upon her face, as if the hurt never stopped since the moment it had been torn from her body. Her eyes were hollow from long-term effects of weather and pollution. A small hole positioned in the middle of her face where her nose should have been made her eye sockets appear in conflict with human anatomy. Graffiti insulted her gown.

"She isn't much to look at, is she? Andy, what do you think?"

Andy was ten years old. If anyone could give an accurate reaction a child could.

"Uhhh..." He looked at me as if he planned to be candid, "She's kind of scary looking."

I would have taken a picture of her bewilderment but I didn't realize my camera was full.

"Well, I'll take a picture of her another time. She's been here for at least seventy years. I don't think she's going anywhere very soon."

Twenty-Six

I continued in my reflections. Derek's dream and everything else about him didn't consume me. He cropped into my thoughts only during the times I had a moment to allow it. I was still busy with my personal life. I had a family to take care of, and I had a job to go to in Washington. When I first got the job, I was put in the job search center for a government agency. It was pleasant work. Within a year I was transferred to a position in an Equal Employment Opportunity Office. In Equal Employment Opportunity, I watched the attempts by the government to balance the injustices of the past with present acts of mercy. The numbers upon the equal opportunity reports represented people whose lives were being blessed by statistical preferences. Those who mistreated their forefathers and fore-mothers ordained it. The white male was left off the Equal Employment Opportunity charts, and seemed to be a standard of measurement for others to be compared against. It was as though he were crowned to be the representative of fair treatment.

My Mormon heritage invited an argument against my employment position. It felt strange to be working in a program that was incompatible with my history and the circumstances of my family. My forefathers didn't have black, yellow, or brown skin, but they experienced much prejudice and persecution even in their pale skins. My forefathers were Caucasian. Their diversity was identified in the form of a religion that influenced the standards of their subculture. They, like other subcultures, witnessed the murders of their brothers and sisters, mothers and fathers, sons and daughters. Their opponents imprisoned their leaders, and mistreated and murdered them. They killed, raped, violated, and stole their properties. My ancestors risked their lives to protect innocent people against the mobocracy that was instigated by their local and state governments.

Protection was denied them because they belonged to a religious body that took a firm stand against the institution of slavery. Joseph Smith, the founder of the Church, documented the Church's stand against slavery by running for president of the United States on an anti-slavery platform. The government in Illinois feared the political strength of this group of people because they were becoming a volatile force against slavery. At the time, Nauvoo, the Mormon settlement at the bend in the Mississippi River, was the largest city in the state of Illinois. The thousands of Mormons that lived there could have swayed the difference between slavery and freedom for many people. Joseph Smith and his brother, Hyrum, were murdered by a mob in Carthage. In the dead of winter, the mobs forced the saints out of their beloved, beautiful city that they had worked so hard to build. Once again, they were driven from their homes, just as they had been driven from New York, Ohio, and Missouri. The only fortunate thing about being driven from Missouri and Illinois was the fact that their men avoided being drafted into the Civil War that would begin after the Mormon Exodus to the west. The Nauvoo temple that had been built on the top of the hill in the city was burned by the brutal mobs.

Thousands of Mormons died in the hardship of their journey to a place in the far west where no one could murder them for their religious beliefs and political views. Twenty-eight of my forefathers helped blaze the wilderness in honor of religious freedom. Bones of my direct-line ancestors became scattered along the way, lying in shallow graves that allowed their dust to mingle with the earth. Great-Great-Great grandparents Whiting died in a cholera epidemic at Mount Pisgah, Iowa. Great-Great Grandfather McCleve died when a handcart tipped over on him at Emigration Canyon. Great-Great Grandfather Roundy drowned in a river. Great-Great-Great Grandmother Christiansen: cholera and starvation. Their names upon a pedigree chart and faded entries in a diary became an example of courage and faith for every child born under their tree. The expansion of new generations and the sting of death for tired ones doesn't revoke the bond.

Working in Human Resources, I was aware of the many job programs sponsored by local and state agencies that were supported by the federal government. There were programs for the youth, disadvantaged women, the handicapped, oppressed groups of diverse ethnic subcultures, and maybe programs that I wasn't aware of. Economic despair and cultural disadvantage filtered into every society, every gender, every subculture, and into every cast of skin.

Derek became one more father who had his heart turned away from the heart of his children because he wasn't able to escape the despair. What forms of survival will a man embrace in order to reinstate his self-esteem? Or, to what will he turn to seek comfort? The options are expansive: drugs, alcohol, and more. The way is open, the options are there. He has his agency. The only way Derek had seen to restore his self-esteem and to find his comfort was to depart the company of his life-long society and his family, for in this particular society he chose to embrace, rejecting your Mormon family members and friends was an edict.

Derek had been nurtured by his father's sacrifice. After his mother's death he watched his father take extreme measures to keep his family together. Whatever it took to bring his children together, his father did. Derek, on the other hand, didn't even know what his children looked like.

Twenty-Seven

Labor Day weekend brought me to Utah. There was business to be taken care of, a daughter and a son to visit, a wedding to go to, a meeting to attend, and a time for going through my father's filing cabinet in the basement of the house in American Fork. I tried to bring a semblance of order to the massive amounts of genealogy notes that my father had accumulated for the last thirty years of his life. I read his journals, and I searched through boxes of photographs. A small photo abruptly jolted my pace. The subject of the photograph suddenly brought me back to the park, when I was standing in front of a dismal statue and Andy was saying to me, "She looks kind of scary."

Not this one. This Serenity in the photograph didn't look scary. It was the way Serenity was supposed to look. My father was standing in front of the statue. He was dressed in a suit and wearing a fedora. Blue-collar work shirts, beat-up plaid flannel shirts, knit caps, and second hand suits purchased from the flea markets were the only wardrobe items I had ever seen him wear. But this was Daddy in his day of splendor. The white handkerchief neatly folded in his pocket might have been the one he spread on the ground for his sweetheart to sit upon as they relaxed at Serenity's feet. I turned the photograph over. Inscribed on the back were the words: *Henry Clayland, Washington D.C. 1934.* The photograph was small and faded in spots, as if the paper it was printed on wasn't a kind that preserved well. My mother had held the camera. My father posed, being careful to stand where he wouldn't block Serenity's face. The camera shutter had captured him for the history they hoped to blend together. The angle of the camera also captured the beauty of Serenity's face and recorded it upon a small three by five piece of paper. Upon the paper, Serenity's face stayed unchanged. The insult of pollution and the temperament of the weather never swayed her look. The vandalism of the uncaring patrons of her grounds never destroyed this recording. Her protected image remained in the cardboard box, stashed away in the darkness of Henry's filing cabinets.

Going through his life, documented and stored in the chambers of his filing cabinets, I gained a new perspective of my father. I began to understand things that he valued and considered worthy to hold onto. The day I spent in his corner of the world was the day I discovered a different father than the one I knew and loved, a man whose life changed in a hospital lounge in 1948. I found a father who might have been able to recover from his grief if the social system had allowed him the chance to do so within his own time frame.

I also searched through another box of photographs that held only the photos that Henry developed from negatives. In the stack I found another picture of Serenity, the same photo Grace had taken. Back in the years when my father had the darkroom, he took the negative and enlarged it and did a reverse print from the negative.

Otherwise, the two pictures were of the same shot, but each one faded in different areas.

The next day I took my father's and mother's letters they had written to each other, his journals, and a few of his photographs. As I embarked the airplane to travel home, I had in my possession the photographs of my father standing before the feet of Serenity. I arrived home with my history in my hands. Forty-eight years after my birth I began to get acquainted with my father and my mother.

Because I had Serenity's true and unalterable face in my possession, I became more interested in capturing on film her current state of despair. Once again, I involved my dear and patient husband in the project.

"We must go back to the park and see Serenity again." I insisted. "I'll make sure the camera is loaded. This time I'll bring the pictures of my parents. That way you can take a picture of me standing right where my dad stood. Then we'll find the gate post where my mother stood, and you can take a picture of me standing there as well."

We drove the Interstate on another Saturday afternoon. We planned to capture a current event that would integrate with my history. It was a great day for taking pictures: blue skies with white puffy clouds. Again we parked the car at the south end and exited our car. As we walked up the stairs, I tried to imagine the automobiles of my parents' decade: big bulky machines scurrying along clean and tidy streets, passing proud-looking buildings and men and women wearing business attire.

Water from the terraced gardens rushed into the cement lake of lily pads. The air was brisk, but there was still an odor as if the stagnant water would never dry up. The trees in the park cast cool but uncertain shadows for the few people that strolled the paths. The park seemed to symbolize a tug-o-war between what once was, and what was wished, a kind of ongoing argument between preservation groups and the government. We reached the top of the water terrace and walked the path that avoided the public speaking platform. A preacher positioned behind a podium held a microphone in his hand and urged the onlookers to repent of their sins. He spoke boldly and with conviction for his belief. Attendance was poor.

Hunter and I walked down the hill to where Serenity was poised in her painful state. We sorrowfully stood in reverence before her. This time black streaks ran down her face, streaking downward to destroy what little dignity she may have had left, as if a vandal had poured a can of black dirty oil upon the top of her head. It was difficult to stand there for very long, but I did manage to fumble for my camera. The movement of a camera shutter captured a window of time. I thought to myself, *Perhaps on Monday someone from Parks Service will wash the insult from Serenity's face.*

Twenty-Eight

A motorist driving through some of the remote areas of Utah might see a few of the people. Her attire is simple and plain. Her arms are covered to her wrists and her legs are covered to her ankles in a gesture of modesty. Her hair is neatly combed, perhaps pulled back into a bun. Her face has an absence of vanity.

Modesty and simplicity capture her spirit. Her humility is for her children and her husband. She shares within the context of her faith. Her husband directs her life and the lives of her sister wives: the women she shares her husband with. If she has no child in her care, she helps tend someone else's children. Employment is not usually an option for her spare time. Her heart is within the walls of her home. Their children's school desks are likely stationed inside the home, where they are taught in a cooperative school system.

Her husband works hard for his bread and the bread of his family. He might have to commute a long distance for his employment, work that is usually unobtainable in his own community. It's one of his many sacrifices. He does it without complaint.

It is easy to look at them and criticize them for their unconventional lifestyles. It's easy to judge them harshly upon the unfamiliar ground of a lifestyle that seems so insensible and out of the ordinary. He may have been born into the faith just as I was born into the Mormon faith, a religion that is still misunderstood and criticized by people who don't know it or are misinformed.

What the situation is that brought him to the community, the motorist does not know. It may have been because of a misunderstanding, an offense of a relative or friend, a bad decision he made from which he was never able to recover, poverty he wasn't able to escape, or an act of selfishness. For whatever the reason, he has found comfort in his habitat and has found friendships that will not fail him. He is somebody's father, somebody's son, and somebody's brother.

A little boy was swept away from his mother for the rest of his mortal life, and he assigned himself a responsibility because of a misunderstanding. A boy lost his retainer. A man kept his mother's songs in his head when he should have relegated them to a place in his mind called acceptance.

A mother had a dream that lived in her head. A woman photographed her favorite statue but failed to say a proper farewell to her children.

Must the traditional primary breadwinner be the standard that is traditionally assumed as always being the stable one, incapable of making mistakes, never having poor judgment or misunderstandings?

Once in a while I will think of my father.

I see a graveyard, a hole in the ground, and a coffin waiting for mourners to leave so the cemetery workers can continue in their employment. My father's journey on earth was finished. He had raised his last child to maturity. It was time for him to be with his beloved.

I see mourners lingering to possess a few last moments with a man that will shift into their memories the moment they turn their backs and walk away.

I see Jensine. I hear what she says when she stands at the grave-site. "If he doesn't want me in the next life, maybe someone else will."

I see my brother Derek in the distance. He is sitting on a bench near the tool shed.

"Come on, Derek. It's time to leave."

"No, go ahead without me. I'm not leaving until he goes down."

Jensine appreciates the love of her children and grandchildren who live nearby. Many friends surround her. Her gardens are fruitful and well maintained. She has won a recognition award from her community.

The wrinkles of age have enfolded upon her. She sees her life as it was since the moment she looked with compassion at a photograph of five little children who had lost their beloved mother.

I see Jensine parting the veil, prepared to step into the next realm of her existence. I see Grace on the other side with heaven all around her.

Jensine sees Grace. She recognizes her from the brown tinted photograph that hung on the walls of her home. Their eyes meet. Grace extends her hand towards her.

Henry stands behind Grace in the distance. It is time for Grace to be alone with Jensine, to say the words that need to be said.

Twenty-Nine

I have learned many valuable lessons since the time my brother decided to embrace an unusual persuasion. I have taken the opportunity to find and reflect upon my history. By doing so I have been able to learn about myself. By researching my history, I am able to feel the love my mother had for all her children. I feel the spiritual bonding of families that holds us together despite a family member's absence.

My attitude about my stepmother has changed. I realized that stepmothers are often the victims of misguided stereotypes, or the victims of the tender feelings of children who can't let go of the way things were. I know that through experiencing opposition in my own life, my eyes have opened and wisdom has been gained.

I am reminded of the blessing of the freedom of religion and the pursuit of happiness. The Mormon religion believes that every person born on the earth, or who will be born on the earth, valued the principle of agency in the pre-mortal existence. The spirits who didn't value it were denied the opportunity to receive bodies in the flesh. God hoped that with their agency, his cherished sons and daughters would act righteously and unselfishly in their state of mortality. He hoped that the choices they would make on earth wouldn't infringe upon someone else's body and spirit.

God is the one that knows the hearts of his children. He who ultimately judges will take into consideration the intentions that Derek carried with him throughout his life, intentions that were impossible for him to fulfill.

I decided that dreams are the stories that live in nighttime minds. The dreamer can make them come true or they can discard whatever dream they wish. My mother's dream was not discarded, and neither was her son's.

I found the face of Serenity.

Serenity remains upon the western slope, undeserving to be included in documentaries on national monuments. As the seasons come and go, her structure continues to decay. Vandals continue to violate. She awaits her fate, not knowing what decisions will be made in her behalf.

She has hope for mankind, for she has seen blind eyes become open, and wisdom gained. She hopes people will have more compassion for any man who has made an innocent mistake, had a misunderstanding, or made a poor judgment.

She realizes that there are fathers who are not willing to give, but are able. May their eyes become open.

She realizes there are fathers who are not able to give, but are willing. May wisdom be gained.

She knows that there are fathers who are not deserving of their children. May the hearts of the fathers turn to the light.

She hopes for forgiving children. For those who turn their hearts away she also has hope:

Behold, I will send you Elijah the Prophet before the coming of the great and dreadful day of the Lord; and he shall turn the heart of the fathers to the children, and the heart of the children to the fathers lest I come and smite the earth with a curse.
Malachi 4:5-6: Old Testament

A family was born at her feet.

(I would like to acknowledge the contributions of my father and my mother: my father for the journal entry and my mother for the letter she wrote shortly after my birth, and for the photograph of Serenity as she was in 1934)

About the Author

Eve Gwartney is the author of two published newspaper articles and one magazine article. She currently resides in Jefferson County, West Virginia.

Printed in the United States
By Bookmasters